This book is part of the Victor FAMILY CONCERN SERIES, a twelve-volume library dealing with the major questions confronting Christian families today. Each book is accompanied by a Leader's Guide for group study and a Personal Involvement Workbook for individual enrichment. All are written in a readable practical style by qualified, practicing professionals. Authors of the series are:

Anthony Florio, Ph.D., premarriage, marriage, and family counselor, *Two To Get Ready* (premarital preparation);

Rex Johnson, assistant professor of Christian education, Talbot Seminary, active in pastoral counseling (sex education and marriage preparation in the family);

Harold Myra, publisher of *Christianity Today* (sexuality and fulfillment in marriage);

J. Allan Petersen, speaker at Family Affair Seminars, *Conquering Family Stress* (facing family crises);

Nancy Potts, marriage and family counselor, *Loneliness: Living Between the Times* (dealing with personal loneliness);

Wayne Rickerson, family pastor, Beaverton Christian Church, Beaverton, Oregon and director of Creative Home Teaching Seminars, (family togetherness activities);

Wes Roberts, counselor in church and private practice and leader of marriage and family seminars (self-esteem);

Barbara Sroka, served on research and writing committees with Chicago's Circle Church and is active with their single adults, *One Is a Whole Number* (singles and the church);

Norman Stolpe, editorial director with Family Concern, Inc., (family goals);

James Thomason, assistant pastor at Calvary Baptist Church, Detroit, (family finances);

Ted Ward, Ph.D., professor and director of Values Development Education program at Michigan State University (value development in the family);

H. Norman Wright, assistant professor of psychology at Biola College and marriage, family, and child counselor, *The Family that Listens* (parent-child communication).

Consulting editor for the series is J. Allan Petersen, president of Family Concern Inc.

ONE
IS A WHOLE NUMBER

Barbara Sroka

While this book is designed for the reader's personal use and profit, it is also intended for group or individual study. A Leader's Guide with Victor Multiuse Transparency Masters and a Personal Involvement Workbook are available from your local Christian bookstore or from the publisher. Leader's Guide: $2.95. Personal Involvement Workbook $2.95.

VICTOR BOOKS

a division of SP Publications, Inc., Wheaton, Illinois

Offices also in Fullerton, California • Whitby, Ontario, Canada • London, England

Library of Congress Catalog Card Number: 78-52782
ISBN: 0-88207-631-0

Printed in the United States of America

VICTOR BOOKS
a division of SP Publications
P. O. Box 1825 • Wheaton, Illinois 60187

Contents

Foreword

Barbara Sroka is the author of the Family Affair Leadership Forum materials titled, "Building a Positive Self-Identity." A former assistant editor of Inter-Varsity's *HIS* magazine, she has a B.S. in Journalism from the University of Illinois and is currently pursuing graduate studies. This book is a significant part of Victor Books' Family Concern Series. In a time of great family consciousness and opportunity, many congregations are devoting increasing energies to family ministries. They have requested reliable and practical resources that speak to the needs of contemporary families. Victor Books and Family Concern have shared this vision and have cooperatively developed this comprehensive family ministry resource for churches.

The church relates to people throughout their lives, and so can help them whatever their point of need. It can teach people skills and concepts for healthy marriage and family relationships with greater depth than any other institution. The church can offer assistance and support at times of crisis, and has built-in structures for education, enrichment, and problem-solving.

This Family Concern Series has been carefully planned to capitalize on the unique abilities and opportunities churches have to minister to families. These 12 books are an encyclopedia of practical family information through which an individual can seek understanding. Pastors and other church professionals will find them invaluable for reference and counseling. Though each book stands alone as a valuable resource, study materials are also provided so that they may be used in church and group settings. As a package, the Family Concern Series offers the congregation a thorough, long-term plan for adult family-life education, and the resources for meeting the specialized family needs of its people.

The resources in the Family Concern Series focus on the needs of three audiences: single adults, never married or, formerly married—married couples, with or without children—and, parents faced with child-rearing responsibilities.

Each author in this series is a committed disciple of Jesus Christ, with a concern for the local church and with a high level of expertise in his/her subject. I am pleased with the enthusiastic cooperation of all these Christian leaders.

God uses people more than books to change people, so this Family Concern Series has been designed to help people work together on their family needs. A Leader's Guide has been prepared for each book in the series. It provides a group leader thirteen, one-hour, step-by-step plans for studying together. These may be used in adult Sunday School, Sunday evening or midweek study series, small informal study groups and as seminars and workshops in conferences and retreats. These Guides include complete study plans, learning activity instructions, visual aids, and suggestions for further investigation and reading.

In addition to the Leader's Guide, a Personal Involvement Workbook accompanies each textbook. This enables each individual, whether studying in a group or alone, to get maximum benefit from the study. Each Personal Involvement Workbook includes the worksheets and activity instructions that are used in the group sessions as well as additional exercises for personal growth.

In studying each book as a group, the leader will need a Leader's Guide and each participant a Personal Involvement Workbook. Even in studying on your own or with your partner, you may want to get the Leader's Guide and start a group study yourself. Use of the personal guide will increase the value of your time spent.

Since this Family Concern Series is a comprehensive resource, the needs felt by most families are included somewhere or several times in the series, even if the titles of the books do not indicate that. The chart on the following page has been prepared to help you find these specific issues in this book and in the other books in the series.

To write a "family encyclopedia" would make for dull reading, but this chart is a guide to the most important topics in each book and works as an index to the entire Family Concern Series. To find what you need, look down the alphabetical list of topics on the left side of the page. When you find what you need, follow across the page to the right, noting the asterisks (*) under the titles across the top of the page. Each book indicated deals with the subject of interest to you.

This simple device ties the whole Series together. It is a road map that can help you get exactly what you need without being encumbered with a massive and complex index or cross-reference system. It also preserves the readability of the books. This chart plus the study materials make the Family Concern Series a powerful tool for you and your church in strengthening your family relationships.

A special word of thanks and appreciation goes to Norman Stolpe. As Family Concern's editorial director, he served as series editor for this project. His vision and relationship with the various authors enabled the concept to take form in reality. His hard work brought the series from planning to completion.

I trust God will deeply enrich your life and family as you study and grow.

J. ALLAN PETERSEN
Family Concern
Wheaton, Ill.

GUIDE TO CURRICULUM SUBJECTS

‡ To be published in August 1979. All others currently available.

	Florio—Premarriage Two to Get Ready ‡	Petersen—Crises	Potts—Loneliness Loneliness: Living Between the Times	Roberts—Self-esteem	Sroka—Singleness One Is a Whole Number	Wright—Communication	Johnson—Sex Education ‡	Myra—Sex in Marriage ‡	Rickerson—Fun & Togetherness ‡	Stolpe—Goals ‡	Thomason—Finances ‡	Ward—Values Development ‡
adolescent children		*		*		*	*		*	*		*
birth control	*						*	*		*		
child development				*		*	*		*			*
child discipline				*		*				*		*
child communication		*		*		*	*		*	*		*
church-family			*		*					*		*
dating	*				*		*					
death		*	*									
divorce		*	*		*							
emotions	*	*	*	*	*	*		*				
engagement	*	*						*				
finances		*									*	
friendship			*		*							
goals	*		*		*					*	*	
leisure			*		*			*	*	*		
loneliness			*		*			*				
marital communication	*	*	*					*			*	
marital conflicts	*	*						*			*	
modeling		*		*		*	*		*	*		*
role adjustment	*	*			*		*	*		*		
self-identity	*	*	*		*		*	*				
sex education	*	*					*	*				
sex in marriage	*							*				
value development							*			*		*
worship									*	*		*

Part 1

The Single Person

1

On Leashing a Lion

The single life weaves back and forth among many dimensions —emotions, professions, sexuality, spirituality, and on and on —always challenging the spiritual sense of balance with a possible upset. It is a mountain covered with a forest of feelings, attitudes, situations, blessings, and curses. It is not an easily traversed plain.

Any one approach to the complexities of singleness, therefore, falls short of its goal. A common approach is to assume that singleness and happiness must be tied together (i.e. you must be a *happy single*). If they are not, being single is unbearable and even pitiable. If one is not a happy single, something is drastically wrong. The single life becomes the oppressor. Without *happy*, singleness is not legitimate.

On the other hand, marriage, even at its foulest, doesn't come under fire as an institution. If a marriage is rocky, the institution is not blamed. "She's unhappy because she's married," or "If we could only find Herb a bachelor apartment, he wouldn't be so dissatisfied" border on being ridiculous concepts. We've internalized marriage as being inherently fulfilling and single life as inherently unfulfilling. Marriage is thought to solve singleness, but singleness can never solve marriage.

These notions sell the single life short. If the single life is approached as unfulfilling or undesirable, it cannot produce warmth and satisfaction. If the approach is joyous and laudatory, it comes across as a clown act. Tears and complaints lead to the conclusion that the single person is bitter and not sold on the idea himself or herself. Anything in between will satisfy only some of the people and be offensive to others.

Why do "approaches" to single living always fail? Because the basic assumption is that being satisfied as a single is inversely related to desiring marriage. The more satisfied the single person is, the less he or she desires marriage; the more marriage is desired, the less satisfying is the single life. Satisfaction with singleness and desire for marriage are not necessarily mutually exclusive, but their sum must always equal 100 percent. If you're 100 percent satisfied with being single, then you desire marriage 0 percent. If you're 80 percent desirous of marriage, you must be 20 percent satisfied single.

The inverse model cripples single people by imposing a *no-win* standard on them. Being a 100 percent satisfied single implies an unhealthy or unnatural attitude toward those of the opposite sex and an institution created by God. Anything less than 100 percent suggests that the single person would really rather *not* be single and that some problems need addressing. This is the classic bind dilemma.

Happily, the church has many healthy, whole, single individuals, in spite of the perceived value of the single life, not because of it. These are people who, on their own and resisting societal pressure, have internalized the worth and meaning of the single life.

In Scripture, both Jesus and the Apostle Paul were fully supportive of both single and married life-styles. Though seemingly a contradiction, this really should be no surprise. Only false values pit marriage against singleness. The model they propose is one of compatibility, not exclusivity. A high view of both marriage and the single life is possible by individual Christians as well as the corporate body of believers.

Is it possible then to be satisfied single and to desire marriage? Yes, though desire for marriage should not overly influence satisfaction with singleness. Their intensities needn't be related. In fact, most singles do like the single life but possibly, even probably, would like to be married some day. The desire for marriage is no reflection on the quality of the single life, and that desire does not have to be an oppressive burden. The reality is that both single life and married life are good and satisfying. No wonder Jesus and Paul could comfortably praise both life-styles.

Paul's statement, "For I am content in whatever state I am" (Phil. 4:11) can be an objective reality rather than an elusive goal—that is, when we learn to accept those problems inherent to this particular life-style and not be embarrassed over their existence.

The irritating qualities of singles' problems are augmented by a corporate herd instinct. Instead of fleshing out solutions to our own situations we're often too willing to accept someone else's solution to a problem, even if it's contrary to our own desires and needs of the moment. We look for the current or fashionable even in problem-solving. In psychology, it's a form of "identity diffusion," where a person will mask or deny individual characteristics in order to conform to the group. Because of our codes, the church is defined as a group of society. In like manner, we are tempted to conform our solutions to the group's expectations and the group's code for handling such situations. This is not fundamentally bad. Though it becomes inadequate under several conditions such as: when we promote only one solution for everyone's similar problem, when the accepted solution becomes antiquated and irrelevant and there is resistance to change, or when we deny the individuality of a person's particular needs. The problems of individuals need individual solutions. They also need the freedom from criticism when accepted solutions are passed by.

The problem with these solutions, as helpful as they may be, is they offer only temporary relief from tribulation because life is a never-ending series of problems. Some of the tribulations of the single life have no final solutions, only ways to grapple and grow. Only ways to develop into loving men and women of God.

Is it legitimate to look at a problem, only to shrug the shoulders and say "there's no real solution"? That's oversimplified. One of the paradoxes of the Christian faith is that while Jesus is the answer to all life problems, most problems of life are irresolvable. We want to boast, "My Lord can do *everything!*" And He can. But when discipleship moves slowly, when God *won't* do everything, and when the same problems remain year after year, we begin to doubt God and/or ourselves. One woman going through particularly difficult times actually lay down on the floor and begged God to take her. Was she slightly disturbed? No. She realized that life becomes problem-free only at its end.

To look at a problem, and admit that the methods of dealing with it don't involve ridding yourself of it, is legitimate. The single life is full of these types of problems: loneliness, relating to people, trusting others, sex, fitting into today's church. And yes, the single life will never be free of those troubled areas of life.

How does the single person deal with single living? There are three ways to grapple with it, three places to flesh out this existence and to learn: the Bible, the church, and within oneself (with the help of the Holy Spirit).

In the Bible, every manner of life is enacted. No one has ever been led astray by the direct reading of Scriptures. God is faithful with His Word, and the Bible remains an organized and delightful blueprint for living.

The church may seem an obvious answer, yet many singles have had to ask, "Where do we fit in?" It is a good question. Those who wish to participate in the church must do two things: let the church give or minister to them, and contribute in whatever way they can to the church. This inward and outward flow runs smoothly when expression of gifts and service are part of daily existence. Yet it is a never-ending problem because the church today is geared to family life, and singles find few ways to express their gifts and give service to the church. The single person needs exposure to every life-style, and the rest of the married church needs the single person, the widowed, the elderly, whether they realize it or not. People become exceedingly narrow when not exposed to others, yet that exposure requires time and effort.

The newest addition to church life has been the singles' group, the main form of outward flow. These groups meet to address the needs of the single's life, at all ages, from all backgrounds, including divorced. Some churches have hired staff members specifically to head up these ministries. Like any special interest group, however, they are not an integral part of the church.

Churches who have groups for singles also find these groups, on their own, are evangelistic. Single people, who otherwise wouldn't go to church at all, will come to the recreation times, discussion times, Bible studies, and informal get-togethers. From there they may come to the church. Attendance like this is so predictable that some of these churches schedule regular times for the Gospel message to be presented. What was started as a ministry to their own people has become a window to the world of singles at large. And lots of singles are at large—47 million of them—approximately one out of every three adults in the United States.

The inward flow, singles ministering to the needs of the people of the church, is more difficult. The first hurdle is believing that single people have something to contribute, so ingrained is the image of irresponsibility and instability. The single person almost always ends up ushering, singing in the choir or assisting with the high school group. Marriage has been equated with maturity. Even the 45-year-old single man who owns his own business finds his set of life experiences overlooked, by others and by *himself*.

A church cannot just minister to a person's needs and expect that person to feel as though the church is his or her own. Christians *must* bear each other's burdens in order to be a part of one another. So, singles' ministries are not enough. They are at best a start and a taking-off point. Integration of church life—achieving a total inward and outward flow— should be the goal.

We have many good representations of the integration of believers. Frequently the union of the Father and the Son is said to be reflected in marriage. The inward and outward flow of all the human beings of a church is also a reflection of that unity. In praying to the Father, Jesus requested, "Holy Father, keep them in Thy name, the name which Thou hast given Me, that they may be one, even as We are" (John 17:11). The reason for this unity is so that the world might know that Jesus and the Father are one. That's a pretty serious reason for being the unified church of God! It is also a good reason to integrate the church.

On the Individual Level

Grappling with single living primarily happens on the individual level. It is what Elizabeth O'Connor calls the "inward journey." God leads one through the pathways of his or her own particular life, which no one else will live—if they dare to allow God to do it.

This is where most singles concentrate their efforts for growth in their Christian lives. For a single person who has no marriage or family identity, being his or her own person, even his or her own family, becomes essential. Going solo is tough, though. God, who sent His Son to live on earth as a single, is well aware of that too.

When discussing the problem of singles and the church, it is helpful to realize the situation is less than optimal but certainly better than the grave deprivation experienced by some

Christians. The Apostle Paul wrote from prison, with joy, but longing to be reunited with the brethren. Dietrich Bonhoeffer, who was also single and spent years in prison wrote:

It is true, of course, that what is an unspeakable gift of God for the lonely individual is easily disregarded and trodden under foot by those who have the gift every day. It is easily forgotten that the fellowship of Christian brethren is a gift of grace, a gift of the Kingdom of God that any day may be taken from us, that the time that still separates us from utter loneliness may be brief indeed. Therefore, let him who until now has had the privilege of living a common Christian life with other Christians praise God's grace from the bottom of his heart. Let him thank God on his knees and declare: It is grace, nothing but grace, that we are allowed to live in community with Christian brethren (*Life Together,* New York: Harper and Row, 1954, p. 20).

Bonhoeffer knew clearly the pain of separation. The single person knows it on a very small scale. This is not to demean the problem. This is to allow us to rejoice with what we do have, maximize our usage of it, and grow to new heights with the resources God has given us.

The first section of this volume looks at the various parts of the single's life, internally and interpersonally. It is focused on taking risks; in loving, living, and stretching one's view of him or her self. The second section is an address to the church; singles and marrieds, pastors and lay persons. As God's people, the church has a heritage that is neither single nor married but one of unity in Christ.

2

Just the One of Me

"Aslan, Aslan. Dear Aslan," sobbed Lucy. "At last."

The great beast [Aslan, the lion] rolled over on his side so that Lucy fell, half sitting and half lying between his front paws. He bent forward and just touched her nose with his tongue. His warm breath came all around her. She gazed up into the large wise face.

"Welcome, child," he said.

"Aslan," said Lucy, "you're bigger."

"That is because you are older, little one," answered he.

"Not because you are?"

"I am not. But every year you grow, you will find me bigger."

For a time she was so happy that she did not want to speak. But Aslan spoke.

"Lucy," he said, "we must not lie here long. You have work in hand, and much time has been lost today."

"Yes, wasn't it a shame?" said Lucy. "*I* saw you all right. They wouldn't believe me. They're all so——"

From somewhere deep inside Aslan's body there came the faintest suggestion of a growl.

"I'm sorry," said Lucy, who understood some of his moods. "I didn't mean to start slanging the others. But it wasn't my fault anyway, was it?"

The lion looked straight into her eyes.

"Oh, Aslan," said Lucy. "You don't mean it was. How could I—I couldn't have left the others and come up to

you alone, how could I? Don't look at me like that . . .
oh well, I suppose I *could*. Yes, and it wouldn't have been
alone, I know, not if I was with you" (Lewis, C.S., *Prince
Caspian,* New York: Macmillan, 1970, pp. 136-137).

Thus Aslan confronted Lucy with her fear and unwilling-
ness to follow him in spite of her brothers and sister.

Somehow, many Christians who are experienced within the
fold of God's family don't have much trouble resisting the
"ways and evils of the world." When it comes to following
Christ, the biggest blocks in the path are fears and an un-
willingness to accept the challenges God has uttered to them,
rather than overt sin. "We are the sheep of His pasture" becomes a command, instead of a description. Instead of
stepping away from the crowd, they continually strive to
conform, not so much to Christ as to any image that looks
orthodox enough, preferring a passive identity as one of the
gang.

In Lewis' allegory Lucy was not called away from drunken-
ness, self-centeredness, or any other trapping of human frailty.
She was called away from following the group that wanted to
rescue Narnia from the evil regime of Miraz, which was a
worthwhile adventure. When Aslan called, like God does, he
expected her to leave a worthwhile pursuit just because he
asked.

When God calls, He calls me to gain all that I *am* and *will
be* from Him. In Christ, I have an identity, that of a redeemed
person adopted into the family of God.

The source of any Christian's identity is, of course, God,
who created us in His own image (Gen. 1:27). We are a
product of God's imagination, called "His workmanship"
(Eph. 2:10). Before any of us realized that we were human
beings needing a relationship with Him, the Lord was pre-
paring a life for us. Our identities were known by God from
the very start. The Psalmist wrote: "For Thou didst form my
inward parts; Thou didst weave me in my mother's womb. I

will give thanks to Thee, for I am fearfully and wonderfully made; Wonderful are Thy works, and my soul knows it very well. My frame was not hidden from Thee, when I was made in secret, and skillfully wrought in the depths of the earth" (Ps. 139:13-15).

What Is Identity?

Identity is that which is you. It is that sense of *I-am-ness*. It answers the questions "Who am I?" "What am I like?" And "Why am I here?" It is practical and workable, not only in relationship to God and Christ but in relationship to everyone and everything else. Jesus said that it's a two-step process (Matt. 10:39). The old must be shed before the new can be put on. This is true. But the losing of one's life has been emphasized so much that many Christians can only identify with the old "lost" self instead of the new valuable self.

In fact, many evangelicals have been taught that any emphasis on self is wrong. "Thinking only of one's self" is tantamount to rejecting the faith altogether. It means grabbing all the goodies of life before anyone else can reach the banquet table of blessings.

But "he who has lost his life for My sake shall find it" (Matt. 10:39) has two aspects—losing a life and *gaining* a life. Self-interest in this passage is changed, not denied. Through commitment to Christ, a precious possession is gained—oneself. Lucy of the *Narnia Chronicles* was called away from the others in the rescue party to gain herself. Each Christian is called in the same way.

What seems easy to forget is that God paid a very high price for each person. Each one is called to great worth, eternal life, and that Life is living in every believer. God traded His Son's death on the cross for our own deaths, and that's an expensive investment. God is no fool. He wouldn't spend a fortune for a piece of junk. He didn't pay that kind of price so Christians could mindlessly perform self-flagellation, and huddle together in flocks of indistinguishable sheep.

After having worked for a brokerage firm a few months, I learned that the stock market is every bit as risky as it is reputed to be. But at least one thing is consistent: People will pay good money if they think a stock will give good yields or good growth. They're willing to invest if they think they'll get a good return.

By this standard, we're worth a fortune; in fact, we're invaluable. God sank vast wealth in us through the sacrifice of His Son. Believers should behave as bearers of that wealth, and show God's interest in self to all those around. In other words, to let their lights shine before all peoples.

Building Identity

Identity is important to every person. For singles, nothing can substitute. Some married people occasionally operate on a reasonable plane, without being conscious of their identity, because of the demands of spouse and family.

Freedom. Not having the responsibilities of a family, singles have the privilege and responsibility of spending time and energy on themselves. The limitations of a spouse don't figure into the decisions that need to be made about home life and resources. The liberty to develop *me* allows for a lot of pleasant exploring and is probably one of the greatest assets of aloneness. It should be prized.

This freedom is often misunderstood as selfishness. But anyone can be selfish—it doesn't take living alone. What is actually being criticized is the single person's self-involvement.

Singles are self-involved, much like the married person is family-involved. Single people need to take care of their own households, even if it is a household of only one member. The single person is his or her own family.

One single person summed it up this way: "I feel it's my right to be *a bit* selfish. After all, I don't have a regular companion, and I don't enjoy a sex life like married people do. I'm asked to give those up as long as I remain single. Why should I give up the good things that come along with being unmarried, like taking time for myself and not having children to care for?"

Interest in self, however, brings certain dangers. Building identity and proper self-interest can easily fall into self-adoration or self-flagellation. Most people seem to prefer self-flagellation. Purporting to be something *less* than one really is causes less trouble and avoids charges of conceit. Others won't object much, even though the continual downgrading of oneself is false humility. True humility is seeing yourself in the proper perspective, from God's perspective. It is recognizing gifts, talents, and pleasant qualities as well as isolating weaknesses.

Prayer. Every believer has the same access to God, the King, as Lucy did to Aslan. In other words, they come to God in a position of strength and relationship. They are sons and daughters of the King. They can pray with conviction because God is their beloved Father.

Karen Mains, who with her husband David ministered with Chicago's Circle Church, often begins prayers with an endearing address to God. She expresses her relationship to the King from the very start. "Dear God," she would say, "This is your daughter Karen speaking . . . "

The Christian's basic identity is in being a child of the King who created him and who is willing to create magnificent works in his life.

Acceptance of and a realistic approach to risk. In her book *Journey Inward, Journey Outward* (New York: Harper and Row, 1968), Elizabeth O'Connor says that the outward journey is a person's travels in this world; the inward journey is that process of continual inward renewal through which God leads each Christian. Though we are forced by our existence to travel the journey outwardly, the journey inward can be resisted.

O'Connor says, "The mantle of youth deludes us about the future. It blinds us to the fact that tomorrow is determined by today. It is now that the young decide what they will be like in middle age and old age. We are under the illusion that rigidity and narrowing of life only begin in age, when actually they begin in the twenties or thirties or whenever we abandon the journey inward" (p. 14).

Seeking securities occupies the energies of most individuals. Those things that are sure are more attractive than something potentially better but with greater risk. Life insurance, a good job, a two-year lease on an apartment, and even marriage, represent security. Yet security in these things is an illusion, for security resides in God. Risk, then, is what we must deal with.

Risk is like a cat, sometimes friendly, sometimes not, and definitely possessing a mind of its own. Only by learning to live with risk can it become a friend. Elizabeth O'Connor, equating risk and threat, says that "threat in itself is no enemy that we should rid ourselves of it. In fact, the danger is that we bar the doors lest it come in, when that feeling of threat inside might be a sign of the presence of God letting us know, if we will listen, that we have put our security in things and places and events and relationships. It is not the threat, but our response to it that is important" (p. 84).

Resisting the forces that would board up rooms of life and freshness and activity requires diligent positive effort and diligent filtering out of harmful negative feedback. For example:

When you smashed your thumb with a hammer when you were constructing a treehouse with your dad, did you conclude that carpentry was only for people who didn't have eight thumbs and two fingers, and never really try to build anything again?

When you hit a wrong note on your clarinet in the middle of the grade school band concert, did the director shoot you a look that made the reed go dry in your mouth and your dreams of performing with the Chicago Symphony flee in an instant?

On my first job after graduation from college, I received incessant criticism from my colleagues about my typing. Later, between jobs, when I didn't know what to do, a friend suggested I try a temporary secretarial agency. What a laugh! I was desperate and tried anyway. I managed to pass the typing test within the "executive" typing range, but that still didn't improve my nagging low self-image. I was convinced that my first day on the job the employer would kick me out the door before 10 o'clock.

Not only did my first employer not kick me out, but she asked for me the next time they needed temporary help. A little bit of confidence, good proofreading, and an IBM Selectric typewriter seemed to make a difference, and for over a year I made my living as a secretary. I took a risk and discovered that I could be successful at something I thought was out of my range of capabilities.

Age. A single person's identity evolves with age, as does his or her married counterparts'.

Everyone begins life as a single person. Marital status doesn't become personal until the late teens, when going together moves on to getting pinned, then engagement. The post high school and college years, and the first few years after college are a transition time. Though most people in this age bracket are unmarried, the pressure to marry is still relatively low (not absent) and there are plenty of peers to associate with. Singleness is not an issue, developing relationships is. The question "What are you going to be when you graduate?" still really hasn't been answered.

In the mid-20s, after attending 10 weddings, 15 baby showers, and 12 bridal showers a year, not only does the bank account grow thin, but so does the self-image. Yet career ambition is high in these years, and in some circles almost everyone goes back for more education. There are fewer marriages, but the pool of single peers shrinks.

What happens after the mid-20s depends on the single individual. Burning ambitions usually decrease in importance, however, and life becomes more settled. The question "Why didn't you marry?" is dismaying because any single person who is still breathing does not consider his or her availability ended. For most singles, the single life is more a rejection of alternatives than a planned event. These are attractive, responsible people, not the drudges and cast-offs of society. In *Ms Means Myself* (Grand Rapids: Zondervan, 1972), Gladys Hunt observed:

Many women grow older and single with quiet good humor and rich lives. They spread love and light and joy around because they have a large supply of it inside. They enter the lives of others with an easy grace. They are interesting, loving human beings who aren't obsessed with their singleness. Men like them; so do women. Usually they have a high calling and are doing what they enjoy.

These women have not let marriage define life for them. They are confident of their personal worth and live with a wholesome awareness and aliveness to the world that belies the stereotyped image of the spinster. No one pities them because their life is wide and full and rich (p. 108).

For these same reasons, some men delay marriage for many years or don't marry at all. In one sense, older, single males are under more suspicion than are their female counterparts. The common opinion, even if not voiced, is that something is "wrong" with the older single male because, *if he really wanted to, he could get married anytime.* Though homosexuality is not necessarily suggested, a domineering mother or excessive devotion to career may be.

In another sense, being an older single male affords a mysterious image. He is almost always considered interesting. He's often in demand for parties. The bachelor image remains a good one, even though not many have opted for it.

The crux of the problem is that the older single hasn't chosen the single life, unless he or she is part of a religious order. Singleness in itself is not offensive, for living unmarried *is* a rich and satisfying life. It isn't deprivation and maiming loneliness. The discomfort is that this style of life is uncommon. Many currently married people never took the prospects of singleness seriously for themselves. Therefore, it is an experience not experienced by the majority.

Little understanding has been granted the unmarried person by the church. Yet God's heart is big enough for all. Shouldn't the doors of His children's hearts, homes, and congregations be the same?

3

Aloneness and Loneliness

"I was afraid when my roommate went camping for the weekend. I woke to every sound. The cat frightened me to goose bumps. I had a knife beside my bed."

* * *

"The beach at Warren Dunes on Lake Michigan's eastern shore-line on a weekday is one of my favorite spots. As I settled into the feeling of the breeze on my face, the sand between my toes, and the sounds of the waves, I began to think. God spoke, I listened. I spoke, God listened. The hours were not short and I was very alone but never lonely."

Aloneness

Aloneness and loneliness are very different beasts. The first person was alone and lonely. The second was just alone. Fear paralyzed the first, who never came to an understanding that he or she was just alone.

All people are alone. Friends, husbands, wives, family, roommates, and children can distract from aloneness, but we are alone. These can provide companionship, and even love, yet they can't fill one's very existence.

God is the closest living friend we have. But by very definition and by relationship, a gulf separates us from Him as well. That relationship remains significant and unique, and is the evidence of our aloneness.

"God is both further from us, and nearer to us, than any other being. He is further from us because the sheer difference between that which has Its principle of being in Itself and that to which being is communicated is one compared with which the difference between an archangel and a worm is quite insignificant. He makes, we are made: He is original, we derivative. But at the same time, and for the same reason, the intimacy between God and even the meanest creature is closer than any that creatures can attain with one another" (Lewis, C.S., *The Problem of Pain*, New York: Macmillan, 1943, p. 41).

Even marriage is no cure for loneliness. In fact, the worst kind of loneliness arises from the shattering of the naive expectation that marriage means no more empty feelings.

To realize aloneness is to run contrary to society's flow of messages, which propel us to increase our appeal to as many people as possible in order to avoid the dreadful alone. Merchants hawk toothpaste, cars, deodorant, housewares, clothes, and even bathroom cleaners to increase "nonaloneness."

The human being desires companionship, and there's reason to believe that this has divine origins. The animals didn't satisfy the needs Adam had for interaction, and God created Eve for Adam as a worker "like unto himself." But even when Adam and Eve were together in the garden, they exhibited aloneness when they made separate choices to disobey God.

Jesus, in the Garden of Gethsemane, experienced an aloneness no one else will ever have to face. He asked three of His disciples to stand watch with Him in that hour, to remain as friends with Him. Unable and unwilling to understand the meaning of Jesus' concerns, they fell asleep. Feel Jesus' loneliness in His word, "So, you men could not keep watch with Me for one hour?" (Matt. 26:40)

Although Jesus, being God, knew that in His greatest hour of need He would be alone, He still craved human companionship.

Yet, each one remains alone. How many people fill hours with exhausting but stimulating busy work? From morning till night, the day is filled. Any break in the bustling causes collapse, even depression. Everyone is afraid to be alone. In her book *The New Community* (New York: Harper and Row, 1976), Elizabeth O'Connor suggests that "much of the fear and anxiety that we have about loneliness is our failure to allow ourselves the pain of experiencing the fact that we are alone" (p. 115).

Freedom lies in accepting, even cherishing, aloneness. Once faced, aloneness provides release, for

in an understanding of your aloneness lies your freedom. The work of silence is to open the door and let in the knowledge of your solitary journey, and in time to make friends with it, and to let it instruct you. Unless one does this work one never becomes fully responsible. One tends to remain what Freud called "the eternal suckling," the one that must always be nourished and taken care of, locked into the precarious, unhappy state of being unnecessarily dependent, and thus beset by fears of desertion (O'Connor, *The New Community,* p. 115).

O'Connor touches on the many ways aloneness blesses the individual. It instructs. It helps you discover who you are. You experience pain of separation and an awareness of the reality of dependence—that it is only mature when you place it on God.

The person alone gains self-responsibility. He is free from being defined by other people. Recently I've decided to live without a best friend, preferring aloneness for the purpose of developing dependence on God and maturity of self.

Indeed, O'Connor suggests that one can never even be an adult until he pursues the "solitary journey." To a child, being alone for even a short time means desertion. If those feelings carry over into adulthood, a person has not yet been released from clinging dependency on others.

The positive result of working through aloneness is that it can become a friend. O'Connor says that "if we can do this hard work of solitude—face and accept the awareness that we are alone—we are in some incredible way given to ourselves. When one belongs only to God and to one's self then comes a peace that nothing in the external can touch or take away, because it is not based on any human being or any thing" (*The New Community*, p. 115).

She goes on to say that peace and stability are the result of coming to terms with aloneness. A Christian released to love freely and to fill others' lives can contribute to the church. Often, however, the church is seen as a "spiritual sanatorium." Dietrich Bonhoeffer warned, "The person who comes into a fellowship because he is running away from himself is misusing it for the sake of diversion, no matter how spiritual this diversion may appear. He is not seeking community at all, but only distraction which will allow him to forget his loneliness for a brief time, the very alienation that creates the deadly isolation of man" (*Life Together*, Harper and Row, 1954, p. 76).

Yet Bonhoeffer acknowledged that believers bring life to the church as they realize the interdependency of their separateness and togetherness. "We recognize, then, that only as we are within the fellowship can we be alone, and only he that is alone can live in the fellowship" (*Life Together*, p. 77).

Loneliness

Loneliness must be distinguished from aloneness. Aloneness is the recognition of being apart. Loneliness is the painful feeling of separation from an unacceptability to others. It is possible to be alone and not be lonely. I frequently take trips by myself. The question always asked of me is: "Doesn't it bother you when you don't have a companion?" My answer is No. These trips are often the only extended time I have alone and they are times in which I reconstruct myself.

I experienced real loneliness for the first time in the fourth grade, when I went to a new school. It was the first time I had to give up friends and make new ones. I was the only "new" girl. I had no one to run up to on the playground the first day. When sides were chosen for games, I was one of the last picked (just before the fat, supershy, or "cootie" kids). Those first few weeks all I wanted to do was go back to my old school.

Everyone is lonely sometimes, but singles suffer from loneliness in epidemic proportions. Cruel jokes such as, "All any single person needs is a swift kick to the altar" precipitate the very things many single people battle incessantly, lack of self-love and self-acceptance. Loneliness, then, is not a condition of physical isolation, but a state of mind.

Loneliness is acute for the single person, and especially the single woman, because daily existence reminds her that she hasn't been "chosen" by someone. Singles continually reside in the shadow of Noah's ark, where "twos" were the rule. Economy sizes in supermarkets either spoil before you've used them or won't fit in the cupboards of your 12' x 16' efficiency. Advertising continually appeals to the libido. When you buy that new $7,000 car, however, that gorgeous model won't drive it up to your apartment complex. No one wants to mess up the seating arrangement at the church banquet by coming alone, so drag along your unsaved neighbor who'd rather be watching television. (Who knows, he might get saved!?!) All pastors have spouses, so do all elders; in fact, everyone who's somebody in your church is married.

The church wants single people, yet because they're a minor proportion of the church population, it's "understandable" to overlook singles' needs in sermons and church budgets. That church populations are predominantly married and older is not a coincidence. What a sad testimony that bars, TM, religious sects, sleep, and sitting around in front of the "boob tube" meet more of the needs of the single adult populace than does the church.

The church, the carrier of the only message of hope in a sick and desolate world, chooses rather to uphold tradition and a clean image. Its people are taught that they are "miserable saved sinners." Thus, they behave as "miserable saved sinners," rarely actualizing the love and healing that relationships to God the King, through Christ the Son, brings.

Initiation and Risk

We're all acquainted with people who, day after day, remain lonely and depressed. It is a self-perpetuating cycle. No amount of activity, no compliment, no amount of attention will shake that veil over their spirits. They are lonely because they can't accept or give love because they don't love themselves. The balance in the love bank account slips to zero and below as the cycle continues.

Christians have a head start on dealing with loneliness because of the love of God. Helpful as this is, however, it is not the solution. One woman, who day after day suffers through her own low self-opinion, said, "I can believe that God loves me. He's perfect. I just can't accept that people would ever love me."

Breaking the chain requires initiative and risk. The former is a change, the latter is a threat. Hard though it is, the single person who is lonely has to take the initiative or repair the problem. All efforts of others will fail. No one can talk a person into liking himself or herself. Even if a person is ready to take that initial step toward liking oneself, a shining bright new self-image can't be polished off in one day. But you have to start somewhere.

In *The Challenge of Being Single,* (J. P. Tarcher, 1974) Marie Edwards and Eleanor Hoover wrote: "We all know the enormous lengths to which people will go to avoid exercising their options. All these avoidance techniques seem to involve the refusal to see significant alternatives to the way in which we are living. We pretend that our hands are tied, that we are victims of circumstances, and we settle into habitual ways of living—ruts—which make us slaves of our past."

You may be a slave to your past. You're lonely. You're dissatisfied with your style of life, yet you're afraid to initiate change. You might chuckle to yourself "I wouldn't be lonely if I were engaged or married." Maybe so. Probably not. You don't know. In any case, that discussion is irrelevant for this minute. You are lonely and dissatisfied today. What are you going to do about it?

You may, even knowing that the cure for loneliness lies within oneself, refuse to move. The old life, as miserable and unrewarding as it may be, is at least familiar. It may fulfill none of your goals, but at least it's something you understand. But can you take the initiative toward success and risk of failure? Elizabeth O'Connor suggests that "God would show us a new land and have us live in a new house, and He churns up the old land and lets the winds beat and floods come. If we are wise and will wake up from our sleep, we will leave the old and build a new dwelling in the land that He will show to those who ask. All the other crises of life that make for upheaval in our emotions have the same creative potential for growth and deeper understanding, but the potential for disaster also exists" (*Journey Inward, Journey Outward,* p. 55).

In viewing a risk, one evaluates the amount to be gained and the amount that could be lost. If the risk of loss is too great, a smaller, easier step could be taken. A woman thinks she'd feel better about herself if she felt more feminine. She decides she's going to buy some bright new clothes, a new designer perfume, and ask that young intern over for dinner

Saturday night. That last part of that bears too much risk because it's somewhat aggressive and it might be unproductive (he may feel threatened, and close himself off). She casually suggests lunch after church one Sunday instead.

The risk involved in the above situation was real. The person who accepts risks needs to also accept failure and rejection and to learn from them. The most loving and accepting people are rejected at times. Even God Himself, the Source of all love, gets rejected. And Jesus, who showed us what God's love is, was rejected, even by His closest friends.

The alternative to initiative and risk is loneliness, which "always finds us frozen somewhere in the *middle:* wanting love but running from it at the same time. . . . It frequently happens that just at the time the prospects of love are on hand we turn our backs and run in fear, even panic. It's too risky. We cannot be responsible for the personal hurt and feeling of rejection if the gift of ourselves is not accepted and valued for what it is. The less we are willing to risk, the more lonely we become" (Ira. M. Tanner, *Loneliness: The Fear of Love,* Harper and Row, 1973, pp. 12-13).

What it comes down to is: me and/or them? If it's *me or them,* then life will be filled with loneliness. If it's *me and them,* then life will be filled with risks, high stakes and great gains.

4

Loving and Losing

All encounters are risks, at least, if they're going to have meaning and love. Margaret Evening makes this important point in a charming volume on single living called *Who Walk Alone* in which she titles her main chapters "The Risks of Love . . ." and completes the phrases. Then she elaborates on the various kinds of people singles love.

Risks, by definition, carry the potential for hurt and disappointment, yet they are necessary for meaning and love. The choice for all of us is to either live with the inevitable hurts or resign ourselves to nothingness.

The biblical standard of love is high. "Beloved, let us love one another, for love is from God; and everyone who loves is born of God" (1 John 4:7). "Love is patient, love is kind, and is not jealous; love does not brag and is not arrogant . . ." (1 Cor. 13:4). We strive to meet these standards, yet so often we give in to hurt, anger, frustration, and hate.

Negative Feelings

Too many Christians gloss over these emotions to keep up a front of "spirituality."

Take, for example, happiness. Happiness is external, puts on a show, and doesn't include sadness. Too often we are pressured to be happy at the expense of expressing sadness. The fruit of the Spirit, however, includes the internal state of joy, which one can experience in the midst of grief and despair as well as in the good times.

But the Christian life does not mean the disappearance of all problems and negative experiences. In *Knowing God*, J. I. Packer addresses the "trials" of life and recognizes the church's frequent whitewashing of the difficulties of existence. He wrote, "But it is possible . . . to play down the rougher side of the Christian life—the daily chastening, the endless war with sin and Satan, the periodic walk in darkness—as to give the impression that normal Christian living is a perfect bed of roses, a state of affairs in which everything in the garden is lovely all the time, and problems no longer exist— or, if they come, they have only to be taken to the throne of grace, and they will melt away at once" (*Knowing God*, Downers Grove, IL: InterVarsity Press, 1973, p. 222).

In dealing with the negatives of the Christian life, it is important for you to "own" your own feelings. You must always be willing to take responsibility for all the hurts that come your way and not throw them on the shoulders of others, even when the hurt is caused by someone else. If you don't, you are a double victim. Not only will there be the first hurt, but the hurt will keep on irritating because of lack of relief. What it comes down to is this: you can deal with your own feelings but you can't force others to deal with theirs.

Essential to every treatment of negative feelings is forgiveness. It is the key to wholeness and freedom. Without forgiveness, you can forever relive the original injustice, whether it was done to you or whether you were the one who wronged someone else. But forgiveness is expensive, as was Jesus' death on the cross.

David Augsburger gives exceptionally good advice in *The Freedom of Forgiveness*, (Chicago: Moody Press, 1973). He stresses that "there is no forgiveness in the cheap little game of looking the other way when a wrong is done. Forgiveness never just overlooks or winks at sin. It does not make light of a wrong. It is no bit of pious pretending that evil is not really evil. Forgiveness is not mere politeness, tact, or diplomacy! Nor is it just forgetting. Oh, you will forget when you truly forgive. But to insist that forgetting comes first is to make passing the final exam the entrance requirement for the course" (p. 19).

Augsburger goes on to say that in forgiveness we carry the burden of our own anger, accepting the hurt that the other has inflicted. The end result: freedom. Is it costly? Yes. It is especially expensive when you ask forgiveness of someone who has participated in a mutual wrong and he or she won't own any of the responsibility.

The Causes of Negative Feelings

Few people have difficulty isolating those situations which need forgiving or have had forgiveness granted. Parents, the church, lost lovers, friends, former friends, and even God bring situations where anger, failure, and grief have to be faced.

The sources of *anger* and hurt vary. One area peculiar to the single person concerns the promise the church often gives unmarrieds regarding marriage prospects. Single women are often told to "pray for the desires of your heart." Granted, the advice is biblical. But it ignores the facts that fewer men than women are in the church and that God doesn't promise marriage. He promises love and fulfillment and meaning but not marriage. So, many women and even men are wounded and angry with God and the church that hasn't fulfilled its promise.

Anger is directed toward others, having its roots in unfulfilled hopes placed in another person. Grudges can be nursed for a long time against a former boyfriend or girlfriend who didn't live up to expectations. One instance or a series of instances over many years may provoke anger. Good marriage counseling releases angry feelings that have been built for years, and may take months to work through. Anger has many sources: shared confidences later revealed, troubles with a boyfriend or girlfriend, broken trust, broken promises, and repeatedly reaching out with no response.

Failure is a self-inflicted wound. It happens to everyone at some point, even the most brilliant or diligent. It is said that Einstein flunked a math course. Failure—devastating single incidents and chronic small failures—is common to the human existence.

The devastating failure of a marriage or loss of a job can shatter daily routine for weeks, even months. People feeling such failure question their abilities and doubt their competency and self-worth. They experience a general giving up, a loss of endurance. And they don't know how to begin again, or even if they want to.

The need to forgive *self* and others is apparent. But it is a long-term process. Almost every accomplished person is said to have had at least one major failure in his or her career. It served as a beginning point for re-evaluation and renewed commitment to making his own life worthwhile.

Failure comes to every life, but it's those negative patterns that are so self-defeating. The person is caught in a spiral of approaching each problem convinced that failure is inevitable. Such an attitude virtually assures repeated failure. Breaking this self-destructive cycle almost always involves a change in behavior before feelings are changed. Nothing will change self-opinion quicker than a series of successes. These successes, of course, will be the result of calculated risks.

Grief is the result of a singular, disarming tragedy—the death of a friend or spouse, a disabling accident, divorce, a broken engagement. The event leaves many questions. "Why? Where's Your love, God? How can I go on?"

During a personal winter period of more than two years,

one well-meaning friend took every opportunity to persuade me to get back on the path of "right living." At one point he even said he thought I'd lost my faith. It hurt to be so misunderstood and to be rebuked instead of comforted.

In times of grief and deep hurt, real friends become primarily listeners—to sobs, anger, frustrations, and insecurity. They avoid condemnation, and offer instead comfort and love. A suffering or guilt-ridden person may need a great deal of love. Condemnation can only destroy him.

The church, often quick to condemn or turn an indifferent back, needs to refrain from condemnation and leave conviction to the Holy Spirit.

Some of those who have experienced tragedy know how intimate the Holy Spirit is. Human compassion may be all around, but no one ministers so directly as God Himself. Matthew recorded that after Jesus' temptation in the desert, "angels came and began to minister to Him" (Matt. 4:11). God takes care of His own, seeing that the basic needs for comfort are available.

After the Winter Periods

One of the miraculous qualities of the Christian life is that winter periods are the very stuff discipleship and deepening love for other humans is made of. Constructive things can be expected to rise from hurts and tragedies.

Hope. Even people in distress display an amazing amount of hope, whether it comes from naivete or a deep-rooted conviction that God cares.

Scars. The imprints left by wounds will forever keep you sensitive to others. Forgetting may mean making the same mistake again, or worse, condemning someone else for a similar mistake.

Great growth. Indeed, winter experiences are a hothouse

for growth. During my own winter period, one friend asked why I thought God allowed it. After some thought and reflection, I decided it was for growth, since my discipleship, sensitivity, and personal resources increased so radically.

Empathy for others. Because of our own scars, reminders of the quality of someone else's suffering, we can give sensitive, heart-felt encouragement to others.

An increase in love. After the hurts have healed, the still waters run even deeper. You learn that God will not forsake you, and that to be hurt is *not* the end of the world. You can take courage for the future. If you haven't reached this point, you probably have not gone through the whole process of dealing with disappointments and hurts.

An increased understanding of Christ's sufferings. In an *Eternity* magazine article, Karen Mains related an incident in which she injured her foot on a garden rake. In her pain, she took the opportunity to identify with Christ and the wounds of His feet and hands. So all types of suffering can be identified with Christ. He was utterly rejected, beaten, denied by His friends, mocked, condemned to die for no reason. The believer's sufferings, especially in the United States, are paltry in comparison. Christ Himself had unusual compassion, and surely it grew from His own sufferings as a human being on earth. He wept at Lazarus' tomb (John 11) even though He knew that He was going to raise Lazarus from the dead.

God can "restore to [us] the years which the swarming locust has eaten" (Joel 2:25). Somehow, in God's sovereignty, His children never waste time. If they pray, "God use this awful, humiliating incident for Your glory. Make beauty and usefulness of something disgusting," He will answer. It is clear affirmation of God's love. Only the sovereign omnipotent Lord can turn the results of sin and failure into gold. J. I. Packer reminds us that "Not merely does God will to guide us in the sense of showing us His way, that we may tread it; He wills also to guide us in the more fundamental sense of ensuring that, whatever happens, whatever mistakes we may make, we shall come safe home. Slippings and strayings there will be, no doubt, but the everlasting arms are beneath us; we shall be caught, rescued, restored" (*Knowing God,* p. 220).

In light of all this, your wounds do more for you than against you. Christ's wounds and the wounds of those He loved become the standard for bearing your own wounds. Calvin Miller spoke eloquently to this in his allegory of Christ's life, *The Singer* (Downers Grove, IL: InterVarsity Press, 1975). The Singer (Christ) is killed on the great machine. He had been tortured, and LIAR burned into his forehead. But He returns and appears before a little girl whose legs He had healed.

Her heart was pumping "Can it be?" and she concluded in her madness, "It is!" She threw herself into the Singer's arms with such a strong embrace it all but knocked him over. "You've alive—alive." She closed her eyes and opened them to be sure that blinking would not erase her joy. "Oh, Singer—I was so afraid. I thought my legs would be as. . ."

"Your's are better far than mine this morning," he said.

His hands and feet were barely recognizable. She who had cried for her own legs was overcome by real concern for his.

"You healed mine!" she said. "Heal your own. Please, Singer, make them well."

"They are well. There is no pain now."

"But they are scarred and wounded. How can they be well?"

"Earthmaker leaves the scars, for they preserve the memory of pain. He will leave my hands this way so men will not forget what it can cost to be a singer in a theater of hate."

"But the word . . . the word they wrote upon your face is gone."

The Singer reached up to his forehead where the searing iron had left the accusation of the council. The word was gone indeed.

"It is," he said, "because Earthmaker cannot bear a lie. He could not let me wear the word for He is Truth. He knows no contradiction in Himself. So learn this, my little friend, no man may burn a label into flesh and make it stay when heaven disagrees."

"But did the Father-Spirit agree with all the other things they did to your hands and feet?"

"He wished they had not done it . . . But, yes . . . He did agree that without these wounds Terra [earth] could not know how much He loved her. You will find, my child, that love rarely ever reaches out to save except it does it with a broken hand" (pp. 141-143).

5

Others in God's Extended Family

Friends come in all shapes, sizes, ages, and marital status. Love flows from one to another in friendships that supplement marriages and families. These relationships just increase the amount of love to be spread around. It is a basic principle of community living.

C. S. Lewis described friendship as "the least jealous" of the types of love. It improves with numbers. As singles reach out to marrieds, and marrieds reach out to singles, they add to each others' sources of love and affirmation. Even married people cannot get all their love and input from their spouses. The general condition of people is that they need stimulus from others.

The young need the mature experience which only years can bring. Singles learn from the models of good relating (and even good fighting) that marrieds can provide. The independent single can help a dependent married person assert his or her uniqueness or can open a window for the world of mothers of young children who may only hear two-year-old talk most of the day. Such relationships are liberating.

The Logistics of Friendship

A single family dwelling just has more space than a bachelor apartment does. If your married friends have children, convenience and casualness is almost impossible unless most of your meetings go on in the married person's home. You can easily stroll or drive over and flop down with the rest of the family in front of the television. It is not so easy for them to gather tennis shoes, mittens, bottles, and favorite toys, and then stroll or drive over to your place.

But there are other ways of getting together. Hire a baby-sitter and take your favorite couple to dinner. A friend of mine used to do this when she was single. She would offer to find a date if that would make the evening more comfortable but made it clear that *she* wanted to be with *them*. I have met friends at inexpensive restaurants while their husbands stayed home with the kids. A little imagination can work into an outing of great fun.

Acceptance is a perennial problem for the person going it alone. The couple who open their lives, individually or together, to the single people help solve that problem. The hugs and touches of married friends qualitatively are not the same as from peers, yet they are important. Their advice and opinions are valuable. A married friend of either sex, for example, can give good, practical advice in dating relationships. After all, he or she has lived through it. And it's an easy way to get answers to questions about the predictable and not-so-predictable behavior of the person you're dating.

Close, family relationships can develop spontaneously through the sharing of needs or church activities. Homes can be places of healing and retreat, though this may be a drain on the family if the guest has great emotional needs. But an open house is a big help to the single person between apartments or school terms. One couple regularly packs the rafters of their house with temporary additions to their family. One summer a young man slept in a hammock in the backyard because there was no more room inside the house.

Those married after age 30 have more acquaintance with single living than with married life, and in all those years, many have developed a great fondness for the single life. One such couple have a ministry to their church in this way. Both before and since their marriage, they've brought more single people to that church than any of the other members have. It may at first seem offensive and condescending for a couple to have their ministry to singles, but the church needs such bridges to be holistic in its overall ministry to people.

Friendships with Married People

In a recent retreat discussion group, the topic moved to relating to marrieds. Almost all of the singles there had significant relationships with married individuals. A few were best friends, but interestingly enough, the close friendships were established *before* marriage, not after. The group generally agreed that marriage inhibits single/married relationships and that the openness of the married people was a determining factor in close cross-marital relationships. Some marrieds feel this too. One adventuresome woman is often tempted to take off her wedding band because she feels that being married forces presuppositions about her. Also, she senses that unmarried folk, especially men, relate to her only on shallow terms because of the "band barrier."

To be able to discuss singles' relationships to marrieds, without having to address the messy subject of friendships gone astray, would be a pleasant luxury. The undercurrents of suspicion and the realization of awful fact, however, make it obligatory. If this sounds like an apology, it is because I feel the need to apologize for the church. The church seems to have glossed over a discussion of this in the hopes that it is only a nightmare that will prove to be fantasy when one wakes in the morning.

Most single women are only slightly aware of the fear many marrieds have that some single woman will steal the attentions of their husbands. They pack their husbands off to work in the morning to what seems to be a much more glamorous world than home and kids.

This phenomenon is amazing, because most single women rarely think about another woman's husband in terms of any kind of relationship besides friendship. They do not want married men. They want men who are free and unattached and relationships that can be all their own, not triangular ones loaded with trouble. Yet it is also true that single women are at times attracted to men who are married, and that married people are attracted to other individuals. Acknowledging the attractiveness of another person can occur without guilt or shame, because no wrong has been committed. Thinking "I'm attracted to her/him" is not lusting.

How do you handle this? To deny that you are attracted to someone is to delay dealing with what can become a persistent problem. For the single man or woman, acknowledging the attraction and accepting it for what it is—attraction—is good. That married person is probably the type of single person you would be attracted to and that makes the situation under-standable.

Your own commitment to the sanctity of marriage is essential if the situation is to remain under control. This may seem like a cold shower. It is. A strong commitment will allow you to appreciate the attractive qualities of a married person of the opposite sex without feeling guilt or shame. Your commitment is a kind of compassion you can extend to a married friend to insure the sanctity of his or her marriage relationship.

When There's an Affair

You can acknowledge all this and even resolve to take it to heart, and still get involved in unhealthy ways. The examples are many and bringing them to mind is not necessary. Rather, we need to explore the dynamics of the relationships.

An illicit relationship usually doesn't begin with premeditated moves. Friendship proceeds slowly and usually without deliberate effort. For loving, caring people, the exchanges of friendship come fairly naturally. It is at a point of need or inadequacy that a person looks to another for validation. Here some pastors get involved with "other women." The woman has expressed needs and, according to Andre Bustanoby, in a *Christianity Today* article ("The Pastor and the Other Woman," August 30, 1974), the pastor takes on a significant other role. He says, "It does not take much verbal or nonverbal exchange for two people like this to become locked into a very fulfilling complementary relationship."

When this happens, the relationship can be rationalized on the basis of "need." The need may indeed be a real one. The deception resides in believing that this other person is the one to meet it and that this is how the need must be met. Once begun, the relationship may continue out of the strong tendency to resist admitting mistakes or real sin. The feelings of foolishness, guilt, shame, embarrassment, and humiliation are crippling, and healing can take place only when the relationship is broken.

The responsibility of the church in illicit relationships is three-fold. The first is to continually provide avenues for all needs to be channelled through, with the understanding that this means of prevention will not always work. The second is to develop loving leadership that can gently bring erring ones to an understanding of truth. The third is to be a community of healing and forgiveness, each individual realizing in all humility that next time they could be the one who has erred and is needing forgiveness.

To condemn a repentant person is as much a sin as to condone his or her illicit relationship. As members of the body of Christ, our commitment to each other should never end. All solutions should be explored. If the loving, healing thing is to let a family relocate, then that should be done with blessings for a renewed life. Jesus knew that the woman at the well had had five husbands and was living with a man to whom she was not married. Let Jesus' treatment of her be that church's example.

The problem of extramarital relationships brings up another. The fear of such relationships can stilt the flow of love and commitment within the church. Rigid rules of conduct will not prevent anyone from entering harmful relationships. Only in an atmosphere of free-flowing trust and affection can a church support and help people with relationships that uphold God's highest ideals. This tension calls for the kind of creativity that keeps us fresh and loving, not suspicious.

The law of freedom, outlined in the Apostle Paul's Epistle to the Galatians, holds. Freedom, of course, does not mean license. A body of believers needs to be in constant dialogue, patching the weak areas and keeping current with each other! The strength of these relationships then becomes a defense against unhealthy relationships and a guardian of the marriage commitment.

Children

No discussion on relating to nonsingles would be complete without the precious little people (or not-so-precious, depending on your orientation). They are people, and significant ones at that.

Lawmakers are finally considering their rights and needs and recognizing their human status. Jesus didn't neglect them, and, as far as "human status" goes, He put them up as examples for all. "Truly I say to you, whoever does not receive the kingdom of God like a child shall not enter it at all" (Luke 18:17).

Children, with their uninhibited observations, relieve adults of their stuffy sophistication. They call the shots as they see them with embarrassing accuracy. A child reflects basic human needs for warmth, stability, love, food, and clothing, and can bring adults back to those values. They are creative and imaginative—and tireless (as any exhausted mother knows). They are whole people in a very special time of their lives.

Children's love can restore. With good humor, their love can bring back the reality that no situation is hopeless. After a great personal loss, some close friends of mine literally took me in hand for a Saturday family outing in Chicago's Chinatown. I was a drudge. But the therapy was good. They kept me distracted with laughs and window shopping. (Do you know that dried fish is a delicacy?) That kind of love, from this family, was healing my festering sore. On the way home, Jennifer, then a three-year-old, told me she wanted me to change my name to Baker, like hers. I could sense God chipping away at the immense feeling of rejection I had. I wondered if all angels were in the form of three-year-old girls.

Being single need not exclude you from significant roles in children's lives. As a child's friend, you don't relate to him as authority figure, as protector, and guardian, but you are nevertheless a model of the single life. If you believe the single life-style is truly viable, you can provide a good example and perpetuate healthy feelings toward the single life. On several occasions, I've heard parents exclaim, "I don't know where my daughter got the idea that marriage is her only option in life. I've certainly never told her that." It's the example that does it. Liberally spreading a variety of adults around can broaden the examples a child has to choose from.

Baby-sitting can be a ministry to parents. If most of your day was spent talking to preschoolers and cleaning up their messes, you'd feel a little harried too. Send your friend to the shopping center or to the library, where she can restore her own soul again. Sometimes you might even send parents on a special night out while you baby-sit free. Regular baby-sitting gives you a fresh look at the complexities of parenting. You may not say so readily, "If I ever have a kid, he'll never do *that!*"

You and Your Family

At some point along the way, most unmarried persons lose their intimate family. They begin to think of themselves as a single unit and not as primarily associated with parents and brothers and sisters. The college years often provide a gradual break from home life. For those who didn't go to college, changing needs and desires in living situations cause many to eventually leave the nest. Some stay home, however, choosing to remain indefinitely with their parents. There may be several reasons for such a choice: the particular relationship is an exceptionally good one; the adult child is dependent on his or her parents either emotionally or financially, or through retardation; the adult child believes God wants him or her to stay with parents until marriage.

One of the most interesting phenomena of parent/child relationships is the growing dependency of parents on children as the parents approach old age. For a few or many years, parents and their adult children have adult-to-adult relationships. Then, one or more children may begin assuming responsibilities for a parent or parents.

In all this, the parent/child relationship throughout life remains a powerful one, whether it is sweet or sour. Most child psychologists agree that a person's basic personality is formed before the age of three. Almost 100 percent of a preschool child's time is spent with one or both parents. That's a lot of parental influence.

People respond to their early years quite differently. For some, childhood was all it's supposed to be: warm parents and lots of friends to play with. Others knew nothing but trauma. In between are all shades of gray. These diverse situations appear in both Christian and non-Christian homes, in wealthy and poor homes, in suburbs, city, and country.

Many people are in therapy because they've never been able to overcome negative parental influences. Parents grip their children's lives in strange ways. Children may move out of the old home, but years of conditioning keep the spirit of mom and dad within them. It is, of course, good to retain the manners and other social courtesies learned in childhood. But there comes a time when single adults need to pull away from parental influences. God does not call us to hopeless dependency or set up rules so strict that we can't break away from what seems conventional. Yet some parents try to make their single adult children feel as though they're deserting Mom or Dad if they leave. Moving out may be very hard and may create overt hostility, but it can and should be done.

You need to make peace with your past. No matter how good your family life may have been, some points will need attention. Coping and facing the past, then, is infinitely better than allowing the past to control forever. The child who was a victim in the past can remain that way or has the option of dealing with it. Reasoning with your parents and expressing love and giving them forgiveness and asking it of yourself is ideal. This is not possible for some. Confronting mom and dad (one or both of whom might be dead by this time) may not work because they aren't at a point of dealing with those things.

Another way of dealing with the past is to accept it as good. Childhood has already happened—for better or for worse. All experiences can be useful. The tragedies and hurts of the past are conquered when their benefits are applied. Though a person may have been a victim in the past, he or she as an adult has the choice of capturing his or her whole life, past and present, to make it rich and healthy.

A Friend is someone you can share simple & silly Things with and never be silly. Thought of as simple or silly.

6

Soul Companions

Of all the kinds of love, friendship is talked of the least. Families, husbands and wives, lovers, and "Christian charity" frequently are discussed, but not friends. Friendship seems to be taken for granted, often not viewed as love at all. It ranks low on the caring list; family, romances, or Christian mission take higher priority.

In comparison with romantic love, friendship breathes more quietly and is less volatile. Perhaps that's why it is regarded less; it is less intense, less adventuresome. At any rate, volumes of literature describe, suggest, warn, cajole, persuade, tempt, rejoice, chronicle—romantic love. No such space is given friendship—except in children's books (remember Lassie—boy and his dog?). Is friendship so dull?

C. S. Lewis called friendship "an affair of disentangled, or stripped, minds" (*The Four Loves,* New York: Harcourt Brace Jovanovich, Inc., 1971, p. 67). In friendship, one bares the soul and its possessions in an intimacy not to be exceeded (when carried to the full extent) in any other kind of love. Friends are trusted with those dearest things and those things that could hurt. This trust is risked because of friendship's self-giving love. Friendship

is utterly freed from [the] need to be needed. We are sorry that any gift or loan or night-watching should have been necessary—and now, for heaven's sake, let us forget all about it and go back to the things we really want to do or talk of together. Even gratitude is no enrichment to this love. The stereotyped "Don't mention it" here expresses what we really feel. The mark of perfect Friendship is not that help will be given when the pinch comes (of course it will) but that, having been given, it makes no difference at all. It was a distraction, an anomaly. It was a horrible waste of time, always too short, that we had together. Perhaps we had only a couple of hours in which to talk and, God bless us, twenty minutes of it has had to be devoted to *affairs* (p. 66).

Aspects and Conditions of Friendship

Friendship begins when two or more people share a common interest. This interest draws them together for a reason; to work on a civil service project, to design the set of a play, to sew a quilt, to study the Bible, to campaign for a politician. At first, the reason they are together is the common tie. From there, the relationship may or may not move on. The relationship is slow moving, with no urgency of any sort, since no expectations are built on the other person. If the original reason for being together ceases, the friendship may stop or it may continue, having been built on ties other than the original similar interest.

Another aspect of friendship is peer interaction. Friends identify with each other on a level common to both. They often feel that the other is "like me" in many ways. Having a peer can bring a breath of relief. That kind of friend can relieve real loneliness which grows out of knowing no one whose life experience closely parallels one's own. A friend walks a similar path to yours and won't mind if you join him.

Friendships contain all emotions and all behaviors. You can express charity, hope, fear, love, kindness, anger, resentment, despair, ambivalence, and every other emotion possible to a friend. Because he or she accepts you as you are, the "ugly" expressions of human living find an understanding reception, and often the mild rebuke only a friend can give. The same friend won't mind teasing and will laugh just as nonsensically over who-knows-what amusement you provide with your childish antics.

Friendship also includes license. You may never make a telephone call after 10:30 P.M. to anyone but a friend. Even three in the morning is all right if you need that friend. As friendships grow, apologies for the small things lessen in numbers, the spontaneous becomes frequent, and efforts to please become more relaxed. Some things that would offend someone unknown are the commonplace in friendship.

Friendship can be shared by more than two people. When others are added, the circle of friends only becomes richer; when a friend is lost, the whole group loses. A group of friends is its own creature, its own dynamic. Friends together pull each person into the center, and create a whole new person. At the end of the evening, it will be said, "We had a good time." If one person of the gang is missing, it's "just not the same without Joe."

Friends, more than dates, marriage partners, business associates, or family, fill a need that is essential to daily life. Without easy access to someone who will listen and with whom you can relax, life grows tense. To have to be on "good behavior" constantly with everyone is quite wearing.

Regard for Friendship

Before the days of romanticism, friendship was the highest of all relationships. It was the meeting of the minds on the "higher" intellectual and spiritual levels. The physical loves, eros and affection, were thought inherently inferior to friendship whose basis was reason and willful decision. Touch was considered a poor second to the intertwining of minds. Platonic relationships, without the encumbrances of physical love, were revered.

The Bible records a friendship of unusual tenacity. King Saul had waged many battles under the Lord's direction, but with time, moved farther and farther from the will of God. The young David proved to be such a skillful warrior against Israel's enemies that the women of Israel celebrated a victory over the Philistines with a song: "Saul has slain his thousands, and David his ten thousands" (1 Sam. 18:7). King Saul couldn't take that and he "looked at David with suspicion from that day on" (18:9).

David and King Saul's son Jonathan met in the court of Saul, when the King summoned David after noticing his killing of Goliath. There was evidently an instant bond between the two young men. The writer of 1 Samuel records "the soul of Jonathan was knit to the soul of David, and Jonathan loved him as himself" (18:1).

In this case, as with all friendships, the one who would be a friend reaches to the other with a commitment of respect and regard. It is a reminder of what almost every mother tells her children, "to have a friend you must be a friend."

For Jonathan, the knitting of souls included love—love as strong as that he had for himself. "Then Jonathan made a covenant with David because he loved him as himself. And Jonathan stripped himself of the robe that was on him and gave it to David, with his armor, including his sword and his bow and his belt" (18:4-5). Even in the most romantic or parental examples, love as committed as Jonathan's for David is hardly ever seen.

Saul's hatred for David increased as David's reputation and popularity rose, and on several occasions Saul tried to kill David with his own weapon—"And Saul tried to pin David to the wall with the spear" (19:10). Saul's attempts failed and, because his son loved David, King Saul led Jonathan to believe that he held no ill feelings for David.

In the last recorded episode of their friendship, Jonathan and David had devised a plan for David's escape from Saul's treachery. Jonathan, however, finding it hard to believe that his father was behind such evil, tested Saul when David did not show for the supper table. If Saul were favorable to David, he would accept his excuse. If not, Saul would be very angry. Jonathan delivered the excuse for the absent and hiding David. King Saul grew very angry, recognized Jonathan's move to cover for his friend, David, and cursed Jonathan for being "just like your mother" (20:30-31; paraphrase mine). Angered, Jonathan left the table and warned his friend David, who then fled from King Saul.

Jonathan's sacrifice for David was great. Their parting reads like something from a World War II movie in which the friendly German girl saves her newfound American boyfriend, only for them to be forced apart because of the war. "David rose from the south side and fell on his face to the ground, and bowed three times. And they kissed each other and wept together, but David more. And Jonathan said to David, 'Go in safety! Inasmuch as we have sworn to each other in the name of the Lord, saying, "The Lord will be between you, and between my descendants and your descendants forever" ' " (20:41-42).

The friendship of David and Jonathan was anything but boring; it was just plain dangerous. Few people will ever have to take the risks for their friends that Jonathan took for David. Yet nothing but their verbal commitment bound them to each other. No wonder their friendship love has been seen as the loftiest kind of love. They were soul companions, sacrificing for each other out of love, not obligation.

For singles, friendship is the one kind of love through which they can express themselves freely. Other kinds of love are either not available (married) or not prescribed (sex). A friend is a friend. That this kind of real, genuine love is viewed so menially is sad, especially since this is the love in which single people can excel. Even the church doesn't always recognize friendship as very valuable. For example, if at a church dinner the seating arrangement at a table allows only an odd number of people, single twosomes will most often be split and moved. Though no one would dream of splitting a married couple, they undoubtedly see more of each other than single friends ever do. Friendship just isn't revered the way marriage is.

Indeed, close friendship evokes suspicion because it might breed "unnaturalness"—homosexuality. It is especially feared among singles because they have no heterosexual outlet for sexual feelings. David and Jonathan's love was real and non-sexual. That's fine. Any two men expressing that kind of love for each other today would certainly be suspect. That's not fine. One wonders what level of friendship could be attained if the unrealistic fears of homosexuality were torn down.

Why are such fears unrealistic? After all, homosexuality does exist. Suspecting every human being of that inclination, or even potential, however, is unreasonable. In one book on single living for young Christian men, the author never discusses friendship, only homosexuality and young men's fears of it. It's as if no other relationship could exist between two men. That's like saying no one can sit at a banquet table without gorging himself, or that a delicate matter could not be discussed without becoming disrespectful with the tongue.

The potential for sin exists in every area of life. Each good and beautiful thing has a perversion of some sort. The tongue praises God; it also spreads the fire of gossip. Sex in its proper context of marriage is beautiful; out of context, it is a source of frustration and hurt. Money when used judiciously brings blessings with what it provides; for selfish reasons, it is wasted on things that will pass away. Even prayer can be perverted. When done with great reverence for God, it is one of the essentials of our relationship to the Lord; when done selfishly, it is just a clanging cymbal in God's ear.

Christians haven't stopped eating, talking, spending money, or praying. Should friendship cease because of the possibility of sin? The one form of love in which a single person can participate fully is ridden with the unrealistic fear that it will likely lead to a sin. Thus suspicious human nature and prurient interests deny the single person healthy, loving relationships which he or she should be free to wholeheartedly pursue. Like any love, friendship will not lose sight of the beloved. The maturity of the individuals and the wise leading of the Holy Spirit are checks against falling into homosexuality or exclusivity. The alternative, avoidance of deep friendship, castrates a type of love which is both satisfying and a source of human dignity.

Developing Friendships

Some people are eternally popular. They fit well in any situation, easily being gracious with one or a hundred different people. Their phones never stop ringing. Others would give anything to have a friend. They knew if they had the opportunity they would, but the conditions they're living in don't permit it. Some examples: being stationed far off in the armed services, or being a medical student without time for making friends. Still others have definite trouble in relating to people through friendship. It isn't that potential friends aren't available; they don't have the ability to make friends. But most of us have friends; close, casual, and otherwise.

Friendship is something we're all supposed to have started working on when we were two, and Mommy first said, "Now, Julie, you must *share*." To feel incapable in the most basic human relationship is embarrassing and frustrating. Tragic as they are, marriage stresses and lovers' quarrels are accepted, but problems with establishing and maintaining friendships seem so adolescent that they are hard to admit.

Shyness is probably the biggest problem for people who have a difficult time making friends. Psychological researchers have only recently started to probe the problem of shyness because it is so common and so often unvoiced. Many are the root causes of shyness. Some people, such as those reared on a farm, have never been exposed to many other people. Interaction with strangers just wasn't available. Hence, the social skills necessary for beginning conversations probably haven't been refined. Others have developed negative feelings toward themselves, making them continually feel inferior to other people. It is important for the shy person to realize that feelings of inferiority are common to all individuals, even the most successful and well known. But the road away from shyness is long.

Developing friendship skills has two parts—starting the relationship and sustaining the friendship. The shy person most often lacks skill in beginning a relationship, though once in a friendship, he becomes a delightful companion. Those who have difficulty sustaining a friendship have problems that would take a whole book to discuss. Professional counseling may be needed to sift problems like these, and I won't even attempt to do so. Some general solutions, however, can be suggested. People who have a great deal of trouble in friendships should realize that all friendships take work and have difficult times. Friendships will not always be sanctuaries for renewal. These folks should also realize that they are capable of friendship, that the situation is not hopeless, and that with work and change, they can develop friendships.

Where Are the Friends?

Simple mathematics allow friendships among singles to break down into three types of relationships: female-female, male-male, and female-male.

Women-to-women relationships are by far the most common of the types of friendships. Evolutionists and social theorists would argue that it's a holdover from agrarian days, when the men went hunting and the women stayed at the camp, rearing the children and raising the crops. The stereotypical reason for the abundance of female relationships today would be that women, ever dependent, flock to friends for solace, advice, giggles, and girlish companionship. Serious observation reveals, however, that women's relationships aren't usually that shallow, especially among women who are sisters in Christ. Besides, "woman talk" is to the female experience what "sports talk" is to the male experience. It may be bland, general, routine, shallow, and interminably boring, yet it doesn't cease.

Single women usually find soul companions in other single women, and less frequently, in married women. This friend is "comfortable" to be with and nondemanding. Single women always have the possibility of acquiring a boyfriend, the relationship with whom might lead to marriage. The woman with the newly acquired male companion may start to draw her needs for companionship from the man who has become her primary human interest. The single friend left behind has to expect the relationship to change. That can be painful. Jealousy and hurt may arise. Expressing those hurts probably will not change the other woman's interest, but these emotions must be dealt with lest they infect other potentially good relationships.

For whatever reason, you may take on others as roommates or housemates. Such an arrangement helps the pocketbook and is also a source of friendship. For any roommate situation to work out, you must first talk of wants, expectations, and compatibility. If tastes and household habits vastly differ, the roommate match probably will not succeed. Money, household duties, decorating, schedules, friendship patterns (a "people" person and a loner don't match), sound levels (quiet persons and high volume stereo sets don't often match), and temperaments all need to be thoroughly discussed before you make a decision about living together. Who knows what can become an issue in a relationship? Most issues though, center around a person's need to be cared for. If your roommate's leaving the bathroom rug rumpled is driving you crazy, it's probably not the rug that is at issue here. What you're saying is, "I'm hurt. I don't think he or she cares about me at all." The rumpled rug is secondary to how you think your roommate is treating you.

Interpersonal relationships always bring their own difficulties. Whatever the difficulties are, they should be dealt with as they arise. "Do not let the sun go down on your anger" (Eph. 4:26) is undoubtedly some of the most practical advice ever given.

There is no truth to the widespread belief that men living together are the clearest living examples of prehistoric life. Some of the warmest, most tastefully decorated, and *neatest* homes and apartments are occupied by men. Most single men are not ill-clothed or in desperate need of a good meal before beriberi sets in. If you're a single woman, having a bachelor friend over for a good meal is still a good idea, but not because he'll keel over from malnutrition.

The "Marlboro man" image is hard to shake—independent, rugged, needing nobody. But that is an exaggerated picture, especially if you're a Christian man who knows the value of close fellowship and the necessity of personal discipleship. Still, many men have a long way to go in learning to express the feelings of friendship. "Big boys don't cry" can be so ingrained that a man might not ever be aware that he has emotions, so well are they hidden. So, male friends are not often soul mates but companions with whom to play racquetball, to study the Bible, to share a hobby, for heady discussions. The individual is second to the activity being done. The "man's way" is to conform to a strict code of social interaction. The product of the meeting and the winner of the competition are more valued than the interaction of personalities. A violation of that code makes those involved uncomfortable.

But Christ opens the door to relationships of superior quality and depth through His love. Being a "brother" in Christ isn't just a tag for those of the "family" of God. Christ calls us to a new life without the encumbrances of the old "code," as unnatural as it may seem.

Being a brother, not just calling each other "brother," involves a commitment, probably with at least some of the characteristics of David and Jonathan's relationship. Those men I know who have found these kinds of friendships experience a release of love that enriches themselves and those around them. Released from the bondage of the "code," they share their lives in a way that brings freedom—both to live and to love. To know and to share with another the hurts, frustrations, growth, lessons, and weak spots is to expand the borders of the human experience, and make us breathe a sigh of relief to have companions in the excitement and drudgery of life.

Male-female Relationships

The male-female friendship is always approached haltingly. The disagreement here is very vocal. The big questions about male-female friendships are: Can they exist? Is romantic love and/or hurt always the inevitable? Is any attempt at friendship merely self-deception, covering over romantic love?

Unless one is very näive, he or she is aware of the reasons to walk on eggs when faced with these kinds of friendships. All kinds of love contain real hurts, but the potential for hurt in this kind of love is seen as more devastating because people risk giving themselves and having themselves returned with a "no thanks." Or, they end up on the other side, giving friendship and concern that unintentionally and unwittingly leads someone on a path to deeper love.

Asking the question, "Can female-male friendships exist?" is really asking if such relationships can survive and deepen without one or both of the people falling in love. C. S. Lewis, who wrote eloquently of love in *The Four Loves,* thought this type of friendship is almost impossible. "When two people who thus discover that they are on the same secret road [to friendship] are of different sexes, the friendship which arises between them will very easily pass—may pass in the first half-hour—into erotic love. Indeed, unless they are physically repulsive to each other or unless one or both already loves elsewhere, it is almost certain to do so sooner or later" (p. 63). Whether you agree with Lewis's basic principle here— that men and women can't share friendship without romantic love—is immaterial to a good discussion. Lewis's generalization, it could be argued, is oversimplified. Otherwise, one must presuppose that every single adult is perpetually looking for the love of his or her life in every relationship he or she encounters. And, once friendship begins, there is no turning back because the erotic forces take over. Lewis doesn't allow for mature thinking and the responsible assessment of self most people go through. So, Lewis is right some of the time, just as all opinions on this question appear to be right some of the time.

Most people behave as liberally as their consciences will allow. They pull the trigger on their own involvement. One man said that it wasn't until he'd become engaged that he pursued any female friendships. He'd thought that all men-women relationships always became romantic, and that had stopped him. Now he wishes he'd made friends with women earlier because he has no natural sisters and had always wanted a sister.

Friendships between the sexes do exist in varying degrees

and forms. The least complicated and most enduring of the male-female friendships are those in which both people realize that no deeper attraction to each other exists. This doesn't mean they see something drastically wrong with each other. One person may be called to a ministry completely opposite to the other's. Ideologically, one may be a conservative, the other a liberal, but the two enjoy the stimulation of each other. The friendship may be one that began when they were children in the same neighborhood or hometown. Longevity and a common experience will make the two lifelong friends.

Male-female friendships mean pleasant comfort and brother-to-sister sharing. My male friends are the ones who hear my questions that begin "Why do men always . . .?" or "What do men really want?" Another pleasantry is that these relationships never lose the sexual dynamic. A person doesn't become "one of the girls" or "one of the boys," just as a natural brother and sister doesn't. It is an affirmation of sexuality—just being female or male. And a single person needs all the affirming of sexuality he or she can get.

As friendships grow, a friend's needs and wants in that same companion could change. An attraction could develop into love. One couple knew each other for more than five years as good friends before ever becoming romantic. In their first years as friends, there was no possibility for romantic attraction. She was a quiet, uninvolved person who had no real sense of vocation. He was social action-oriented, participating in the civil rights movement from the very first and was committed to a city ministry. She was the one who changed, gradually assuming a love for the poor and oppressed and feeling that the city was where she'd like to invest her life.

Male-female relationships become complex when one person grows to love the other and that love is not reciprocated. Precisely this fear keeps many women and men from even pursuing friendships with the opposite sex. But the hurts and disappointments of love are facts of a love-filled life. It's not *Will it happen?* but *What will you do when it does?*

When one friend's feelings turn to love, the relationship changes even if the other person's feelings haven't. There are new conditions. The only *must do* here is talk, for that at least, keeps everything in the open.

The "friend" friend may come around to loving the "lover" friend. One woman finally realized that God wanted her to marry the man who'd been pursuing her. He was just perfect for her, but she didn't particularly want to get married. She was having too much fun as a single person. (Incidentally, she was 32 at the time.) Marriage was a good decision for her.

In another instance, a man was afraid to make a commitment beyond friendship. His girlfriend couldn't take his indecision any longer and confronted him with, "Don't you have *any* feelings for me?" He did, and acknowledged them.

Such fairy-tale endings don't always happen. A relationship may finally break off because it becomes too trying or the "friend" friend finds a romantic interest.

A lot of feelings developed over those months of friendship. Now the "lover" friend must take responsibility for his or her own feelings. No one *forced* those feelings to grow. It was a decision made at some point by a loving, giving person. And that can't be held against the other person (unless the other person played with feelings). For the "friend" friend, it's important to help the other person through by talking, being honest and caring, and knowing the appropriate time to split. Because, in the end, the "lover" friend has to be alone.

The person whose love is not reciprocated has much internal work to do. Feelings of rejection and failure work at destroying self-image, making one wary of getting involved again. Most important to healing is recognizing God's love has never changed. Secondly, the "lover" friend needs to respect himself or herself for daring to love. Whether it was returned or not, it was a precious gift and the bearer should be glad he or she is a warm and loving person who is capable of that depth of feeling.

Another positive is the opportunity to grow through suffering. Peaceful, spirit-filled natures are not honed by easy living. Remember, "We also exult in our tribulations; knowing that tribulation brings about perseverance; and preseverance, proven character; and proven character, hope; and hope does not disappoint; because the love of God has been poured out within our hearts through the Holy Spirit who was given to us" (Rom. 5:3-5).

An appropriate prayer might be, "God, I hurt terribly right now. And sometimes I think I even hate. But take this burden of mine and fashion a greater loving person because of this experience." You can't be blamed for thinking that it's impossible to pray a prayer like that. But, hurt is the calculable risk of love. Those who face and conquer the hurt, enduring the pain of cleaning a wound, go on to be *more* loving people. Those who don't, remain in a pit of hurt, self-pity, lovelessness. Their wounds remain unhealed because they won't face the pain of cleansing.

Risking love and enduring pain is the process of maturing. A Christian psychiatrist summarized it this way: "Christian patients have told me, after a long struggle with some emotional problem, that they realize they have become stronger, have learned more about God, and have become better equipped to lead a constructive Christian life. This growth is not *in spite of* their emotional problems, but *because of* the process they have gone through in finding relief" (James D. Mallory and Stanley C. Baldwin, *The Kink and I: A Psychiatrists Guide to Untwisted Living,* Wheaton, IL: Victor Books, 1974, p. 53).

The third option for unrequited love is to remain in the uneven relationship indefinitely, always hoping that the other person will change. Indeed, this relationship, because of the changing nature of individuals, may grow away from love.

Without fireworks, the "lover" friend loses interest. Those who remain in this type of relationship may find it rewarding, even if not completely satisfying, for love is somehow always returned.

The key to any love relationship is to remain fresh. It is the Christian's privilege to be interminably related to the Creator and Source of all love—God. Love, no matter how or what, is always being poured into the life of the believer. That is security. That is low risk. God loves. Then "we love, because He first loved us" (1 John 4:19).

7

Dating Redeemed

In my opinion, dating, in Christian circles, is a collosal atrocity. It's Watergate, My Lai, and the Syndicate over dinner. As an institution, dating is built on poor teaching, fairy-tale stories of knights and princesses, sexual misunderstanding and frustration, incredible pressure to get married, and the genuine need to express love to others, which often ends up a flower growing in a garbage dump.

The main worldly aspect in dating is the incredible pressure we put on people to perform—to build our egoes and self-images, even to prove what kind of marriage partner the other would make. It's almost an acceptable form of selfishness.

For those who have transcended beyond that selfishness, dating becomes a mutual exchange, characterized mostly by fulfilling experiences, not misread intentions or broken hopes.

Dating Defined

Not long ago I realized my ideas on dating from my youth were a fantasy built on the Cinderella story. In kindergarten, almost every day I went to the bookshelf and read how beautiful Cinderella was hated by her stepmother and ugly sisters. The story was supposed to teach young children that beauty of spirit, not haughtiness, gained reward. Cinderella's reward was marriage to the handsome prince, a life lived happily ever after in his castle. I did learn the appropriate virtue, but I also believed that someday *my* handsome prince would come and sweep me away. All I had to do was be a good girl.

The preconceived ideas of how it's "supposed" to happen carry a lot of grief because they are leftovers from youthful dreams and images. They are the leftovers of playing bride and house, of watching Marlon Brando in *A Streetcar Named Desire,* of hearing Mommy or Daddy say, "Of course you'll get married some day."

Once, after delivering the "happy and single" talk at a Christian camp, I was told my message was good, but that's not where the college students were at. I talked about accepting aloneness, developing an identity, learning to love all kinds of individuals, grappling with sexual desires. What they wanted to hear was how to develop good relationships with the opposite sex. Not more than one-half of them would marry in the next four years, but they wanted to know how to give up the single life, not how to live it.

A friend of mine recently struggled with this same problem. He was asked to develop and conduct for some college students a one-day seminar on single living. He knew what he wanted to say (he was in his late 20s) but he also knew what the students wanted to hear and that they most likely wouldn't listen to what he wanted to say. Almost everyone has been brought up to get married. This is what they're told is supposed to happen, and this is what they're after.

One respected and popular author states that a Christian young person's goal should be marriage by the age of 23. He says, "For a boy to 'date the field' until he is age twenty-one to twenty-five indicates the existence of major emotional problems" (Herbert J. Miles, *The Dating Game,* Grand Rapids: Zondervan, 1975, p. 54). In that case, a lot of us are in trouble.

As the single person grows older, things change, the remnants of peer pressure leave, and he or she is usually able to accept being alone, and doesn't need a relationship to define him or her. The older single has developed more identity, and looks to possible mates less with a desire to find someone to *complete* him or her but to *complement*. Social "codes" don't mean as much and the older single is less likely to play games, less likely to wonder if "kissing on the first date is wrong."

The meaning of *dating* even changes. People spend time with each other, and get to know each other, and then "go" with someone. Maybe it's because the word brings up all kinds of silly images, like the senior high social and sodas in the malt shop, or we think we'll be on trial to perform. One friend of mine says she can't "date" because it puts all kinds of pressure on her. But she does go out with men.

Your Own Worth

Personal worth can suffer considerably in the dating process. You want to be attractive and pleasant, but find it difficult not to succumb or react to the media image of an attractive male or female. Dowdy clothes have nothing to do with chastity, only with a restricted view of it. Kindness and consideration of others should characterize your approach to clothing, style, and modesty. Cleanliness and a sunny disposition all show self-respect, as do personal investments such as education and recreation. The man or woman of God is eager to know what kinds of gifts the Lord has given and is eager to put them to use. God will create an interesting, unique you, if you'll let Him.

If you're a woman, this is especially important for you to realize. Women will often settle for much less than what they're worth and will too readily believe that they are inferior. As far as getting married is concerned, a woman may settle for any man rather than no man at all. "Wait for God's best" has become cliché.

Wait for the best of everything, since marriage is promised to no one. If the best doesn't include a husband, then accepting that is necessary. Realizing that older single women (and men) aren't failures is also necessary. The idea that marriage is the highest reward is a false one. Marriage is no trophy at all in the kingdom here on earth, though that is almost impossible to believe by the unquestioning way we accept married life as superior to single life.

If you're a single man, you'll have to get over the idea that women want to be impressed. Jesus impressed women, but He impressed them with His love, not with masculine tricks or lists of degrees and awards. Jesus always had productive giving relationships with women. They flocked to Him. He was such an exceptional man. In each encounter with women He built the personal worth of the individual: with the Syrophoenician woman, with Mary, with Martha, with Mary Magdalene, with His own mother, with Joanna, with the woman at the well, and "many others who were contributing to their support out of their private means" (Luke 8:3). He never lost sight of their value. He appreciated, corrected, and encouraged. He wasn't afraid of touch when His feet were bathed by the weeping prostitute in front of the temple elders. And, most of all, He didn't discourage them from loving Him.

Finally, you should allow yourself the privilege of failing and succeeding. The human condition says you will make mistakes, some of which will be perfectly charming on occasions. Laugh and rejoice together.

The Worth of Others

The flip side of personal worth is worth of others. Believing in anything else is the root of exploitation, the abuse of others for personal gain. And in dating, it's possible to be exploitive, even while following all the rules of good conduct.

Granting the worth of others is more than respect; it's a celebration of God living in another individual—worship to God for His love shown in the creation of humans. Celebrating the personal worth of the other individual on a date will do several things. It will:

encourage you to be deeply interested in all aspects of that person's life;

create a servant attitude for that evening;

increase love feelings, which may or may not be romantic;

make whatever physical expression that takes place into an expression of that worth;

encourage you to relax and just enjoy; and

allow spontaneity since rigid standards and rules haven't been set.

At least two things will destroy all your efforts at celebrating the worth of another person: (1) rating that person on your handy-dandy marriageability chart and (2) expecting real concern to *necessarily* blossom into true love.

Praying for the other person *before* the date can help you focus on the worth of the other person. It takes just 10 minutes to address God about the needs and concerns of the other, how they might be met that night, and for a genuine evening of fun.

What Should You Expect on a Date?

What kinds of mature things can you expect from dating? You can expect fun, respect, friendship, sharing Christ in you. You can learn about the opposite sex and about what could or could not be good for you in marriage. You can (or should) expect some affirmation of your womanhood or manhood.

You can't expect to get married. You may have been taught that somewhere, sometime, *The One* will arrive on the scene. Not necessarily so. Marriage may be the culmination of your dating but it is not the purpose or the inevitable end of dating. A promise of marriage is cruel and unusual pressure on what is otherwise an excellent way for a single person to express humanity.

Dating always aimed at marriage is just a game of "prove yourself." Dating for fun is your gift to each other. The difference is in intention and purpose, though the results will probably be similar. The same number of people will probably get married, but with any effort, maybe there won't be so many casualties—those who feel they've failed and are second-class sexless objects.

Sex and Sexuality

Sexuality and its expressions are two of the most popular subjects of any book or column. The problem is, if you listened to all the advice of all the books and articles, you would be more confused than ever, so contradictory are the messages. No one could follow all the advice.

For the purposes of definition, sex is what one does, sexual expression is the way one lives his life. With Scripture prohibiting sex (the physical act) outside of marriage, most singles have to participate in sexual expression. Sexual expression starts in fully being a woman or a man, but that doesn't mean any stereotyped macho or southern belle image. You are a sexual being, and your sexual expression will be what you make of it. Start with liking yourself as the sex you are. One female friend of mine spent more money than she probably should have on a perfume she liked because it made her feel very feminine and she liked that feeling. In my opinion, that was a good investment.

One of the most confusing messages of the church concerns sexuality. Many Christians are so uptight about sex and sexuality that they approach a good thing as if it were leprosy. They're afraid of it before they even know what it is. They see the entrapments and evils of abuse first. Only when a sufficient amount of cold water has been thrown on their heated bodies do they hear that sex and sexuality is good and created by God. The approach is backward. Instead of seeing the good and positive, we immediately focus on the negative evil view.

Most arguments within the conservative approach to sex and sexuality ring with such questions as "Aren't we playing with fire?" Yes, but fire cooks food and creates warmth and gives light. Just because you might get burned is no reason to be cold and hungry, and to sit in the dark. Sexuality does have dangers and risks. But instead of denying it, shouldn't Christians spend time learning the healthy and biblically acceptable ways for single people to express physical affection? The church needs to view physical touch and warm verbal exchanges as something good and enjoyable for all people, but varying in degrees for the single and the married.

Every person has a sexual philosophy. Some of the general standards by which people express their sexuality are:

(1) *Don't!* You can look (not too hard) but don't touch! Some don't even believe in premarital handholding. The problem here is steam-kettle buildup, and what to do with normal sexual feelings.

(2) *Hedonism.* If it feels good, do it. This isn't a serious option for the Christian who respects the opposite sex.

(3) *Go as far as you can without getting into trouble.* This is what parents fear the most, but it is not a real problem for the casual dater. This is a loaded gun, one slip and you've had it. The question here is: Why are you doing this in the first place? Is it because you're lonely?

(4) *Some sexual expression only if it's serious.* There is none in friendship or casual dating. The problem here comes in defining which relationships are serious, and that puts the pressure on for a decision.

(5) *Everything in moderation.* This philosophy permits sexual expression according to where you and your friend are. This involves thought and consideration as to where the other person is. The accusation here is that sexual expression is taken too lightly, and thus is not so special.

(6) *He pays now, she pays later plan.* Even though a man might not want much, most women are offended by this standard. It's a few rungs down the ladder of ill-repute. If you can't change the man, then make sure you at least pay for half the expenses incurred on the date.

In any exchange of physical expression, care must be taken. You may be perfectly clear as to what a good-night kiss means, but your intents may not be so obvious to the other person. The need to talk about your expressions is real, even on a first date, if need be. People interpret physical actions according to their own standards, not the ones their friends are coming from. To be honest is only fair.

Masturbation (sex with yourself) has been talked about a lot lately. It should come out of the closet and I hope no one still believes that insanity will befall you if you masturbate. While the Bible doesn't say anything specific about masturbation, it's sex outside the optimum situation.

An Approach to Sexual Expression

You shouldn't assume that you need to adopt a particular approach to sexual expression just because "everyone is doing it" or the local pastor believes in it. Adopting your own approach involves a decision-making process of three questions: Where are you now? Where do you want and need to be? How are you going to get there?

These questions center on recognizing your own situation, evaluating it, then acting on it. This is tough. It may mean thinking about something you don't want to think about. It may seem very unromantic. But the time to make decisions about values is before you're faced with a compromising or puzzling situation. The middle of a long embrace is no time to think about whether you really want to do it or not. On the other hand, racing to the door at the end of the evening without looking back won't convince your date you'd like him or her to know how you feel.

So, the answers to the three questions should be pleasing to you, pleasing to God (admittedly sometimes hard to determine), honorable to those people around you, and pleasing to those people around you (especially the opposite sex). How might these answers be expressed? Here are a few hypothetical situations:

Do you feel that you need to pull completely away from sexuality and sex because you were trying to make sex fill your loneliness needs? Maybe *Don't!* is your best solution for now. Perhaps your decision would be to live with *Don't!* for six months to get your head back on straight.

You're shy. No man has ever looked at you twice. You have literally been sexless. How do you begin expressing sexuality? Perhaps you should buy a new outfit in a *bright* color, decidedly of the image you would want to be—not a sexy vamp, but a poised woman. Then, accept all the compliments. Practice looking at people, especially single men, straight in the eye and saying, "Thank you." Then, smile.

You've never really dated much but know that one day you'd like to marry. Plus you don't see anyone interesting right now. Lately, you've wondered whether your expectations are too high. Besides, you wouldn't know what to do with the man or woman of your dreams if you met him or her, you're so inexperienced in social situations. So, you go with or ask someone out in order to have a good time and learn some more about the opposite sex.

Why is it necessary to say these things? Because a huge number of people are locked into unproductive behavior.

Single people can go on for months and years knowing that something must change if sexual expression is to be satisfying, yet they don't know how to change, they don't want to change, or they're afraid to change. The easiest decision to make is to make no decision at all.

One of the bigger problems is misread intentions. You may be shy about reaching out to others of the opposite sex because you fear that some level of sexual expression may be interpreted as something more or less than what you want it to mean.

Well, if you can express it with a kiss, then you can express it with your mouth. Talk about it! This may seem silly or stilted, but it's not. Talking will be a big relief. When you hold hands, at some point say, "I appreciate you. I want to express this to you, this is what it means. This is where I'm at." Your frankness may surprise your companion, but you'll probably be able to read "thanks" in his or her response. You might also ask, "What can you handle right now? Will kissing you create problems, rather than be a pleasant experience?"

Another area of misunderstanding is touch. Psychologists realize the necessity of touch. Babies die without it. So do adults, though they die internally.

The Apostle Paul recognized the importance of human touch. On several occasions, he saw fit to remind the brethren to "greet one another with a holy kiss" (Rom. 16:16; 1 Cor. 16:20; 2 Cor. 13:12; 1 Thes. 5:26). In today's reserved church, probably the most we could muster would be a holy handshake or maybe a holy embrace.

Touching is an expression of pure warmth. In dating, touch is a healthy way of affirming another person. Once, during the refreshments time of a meeting, one of the men there walked by me and, on his way past, reached out and patted my stomach. That's quite different from a hand on the arm or the shoulder. But I was amused and pleased—and surprised. This man knows the joy of touching.

You and Others

You don't live in isolation, neither do you date in isolation. If you and your dating partner attend the same church, other people in the church will probably know about the relationship if it's gone on for any time or is very serious. This can bring its own pack of troubles because the only involvement the rest of the church has had in the dating lives of single people is to speculate and gossip. At times it almost resembles an evangelistic campaign. Couples who really don't know what stage their relationship is in find people making their wedding plans for them. In her book *Who Walk Alone* (Downers Grove, IL: InterVarsity, 1974), Margaret Evening pleads "that other friends leave single people to enjoy friendships between the sexes without speculating, gossiping, interfering, or commenting. Allow relationships to take their own course, and deepen of their own accord. Rejoice, encourage and, if asked, advise, but never try to manipulate the lives of others. This can be a dangerous game to play and, in any case, it is really the prerogative of Almighty God, who *alone* can 'order the unruly wills and affections of sinful men' " (p. 70).

Health and wholeness should be encouraged, even from the pulpit. The church must allow the single person the freedom to move in and out of relationships, without criticism or meddling. And, when the inevitable hurts happen, the church should be a place of healing and love. Breaking off a relationship hurts enough without people gossiping and not taking the hurt seriously.

In some churches, single people who begin dating are encouraged to take that dating relationship to the church elders for counseling. The couple is discipled throughout the relationship. This usually happens only if there is a strong authority structure. Knowing that decisions can be made with good counsel adds security. The biggest positive in groups where this can happen is that the whole church is involved in the process.

The whole topic of interpersonal relationships between the sexes is always a sticky one. One psychologist summed it up beautifully: "We need to view ourselves as whole persons. Whatever brings health and wholeness to your experiences with the opposite sex should be pursued. You owe it to yourself."

8

Home Sweet Apartment

Homes aren't the only places where hearts are. Apartments, dorm rooms, and one-room efficiencies can be as warm and friendly as a toasty fire. Friendship expressed through hospitality happens wherever the willing host or hostess lives, no matter what the quarters or the resources. No one will notice that he's drinking lemonade out of a Ronald McDonald cup or that the "silver" is plastic if the home environs repair fractured days, settle jangled nerves, or make him laugh until his sides ache.

The church often views singles as recipients of hospitality, not practitioners. They're the ones asked to bring the rolls, not a hot dish, to the church potluck. The single life breeds images of domestic incompetency: crates for furniture, TV dinners, mattress on the floor, and a $2,000 stereo set with components. Any serious entertaining is done out because singles (1) don't have the time to plan and cook, (2) don't have the money, (3) aren't interested in hospitality, and (4) don't know *how*. One 35-year-old single woman complained, in all seriousness, that "people seem to think that just because I live by myself, I never get a good meal."

Not only does the church view the single in this way, but many singles view themselves in this way. It isn't that they never have guests, but they limit their scopes to peers, family, or married couples of similar ages. I've heard it said, "I'd love to have 'So-and-sos' over after church on Sunday, but they have kids." That requires more thought—food that children enjoy, having things for the kids to do, asking Mom and Dad to bring the high chair or portable crib, and child-proofing the apartment.

What Is Hospitality?

Hospitality is more than feeding and sheltering the people who walk through your apartment door. It is a state of heart —those things that turn a guest into a friend. In *Open Heart-Open Home* (Elgin, IL: David C. Cook, 1976) Karen Burton Mains distinguishes between entertaining and hospitality in this way: "Secular entertaining is a terrible bondage. Its source is human pride. Demanding perfection, fostering the urge to impress, it is a rigorous taskmaster which enslaves. In contrast, scriptural hospitality is a freedom which liberates.

"Entertaining says, 'I want to impress you with my beautiful home, my clever decorating, my gourmet cooking.' Hospitality, however, seeks to minister. It says, 'This home is not mine. It is truly a gift from my Master. I am His servant and I use it as He desires.' Hospitality does not try to impress, but to serve" (p. 25).

By Karen Mains' criterion, one room in a dormitory residence can be a lovely home.

Hospitality is several things, all of which emphasize comfort over entertaining. It is the sharing of quarters with friends and relatives. One may not have a guest room, but clean sheets on the bed for a guest and spending one night on the sofa doesn't hurt. The apartment in which I live has a large living room which can become a private room. There's no frill or flair, but it's comfortable and spacious, and in a four-room apartment, that's not bad.

Hospitality also includes providing a place for the Lord's work. Meetings can be held anywhere there are enough coffee mugs and comfortable chairs (for those who want them). A place dedicated to the work of the Lord always accomplishes what it has been set aside to do. I'll never forget those days in the dorm, when we'd meet for prayer in someone's 8′ x 10′ room. Four people on each bed, people propped up on pillows on the floor around every square inch of wall, and a few chairs. There was always enough space.

Hospitality is spontaneous. That means warmly welcoming anyone at the door into the very heart of the home, even if it is strewn with newspapers and the rug hasn't been vacuumed in two weeks. Isn't it pride that really makes people not want others to view them as they actually are?

Hospitality is fun. Any kind of party relaxes the muscles and allows people to meet. A night of table games, pulling taffy, just sitting around talking while listening to music, or hot chocolate breaks at 10 o'clock. Teachers I know have spent the night grading papers together, then gone out for ice cream when they were done.

Dimensions of Hospitality

Hospitality is not just a good idea; it is a command. In his letter to Timothy, Paul lists hospitality as one of the requirements for office in the church (1 Tim. 3:2). The Apostle Peter encouraged Christians to "be hospitable with one another without complaint" (1 Peter 4:9). Church life includes using one's very resting place in service to God.

An important principle is *do with what you have*. True hospitality is not a strain on a budget, though it might stretch it a bit. So what if you have only four glasses and eight are coming for a meeting. Borrow, wash, and return. Maybe you've just had a good bike ride and you and your companion are ravenously hungry. Is the cupboard really bare? Think. If you put this with that and add those.

You're strapped. Payday is Friday, and today is Wednesday. All you need is one more thing to round out that evening. Get on the phone and ask one of your guests to stop at the store on the way over.

The same principle applies to decorating. Some think good stewardship means denial of any creature comforts. Others won't let anyone through the door unless the place looks like something out of *Apartment Life* or *Better Homes and Gardens*. Home is where you're comfortable and any way you accomplish that meets the criterion.

For years, a woman has opened her home to a myriad of American and international visitors. Being invited to dinner there can mean anything from an Indian menu to after dinner entertainment on Chinese musical instruments. Her zest and flair make it an exciting place where people keep stopping by. The laughter and light heart of this person radiates and warms her house.

Unfortunately, hospitality has been segmented. At no place more than at a dinner party is one reminded that two is even, one is odd. Couples will invite other couples, but to break that multiple of two seems very hard.

In relationship to maintaining the household of God, we must use every possible method to overcome those things which divide. Sunday morning services and church picnics don't allow the time nor the exclusivity to empathize with each other. Yet rarely does anyone initiate further getting together. One-to-one exchanges, no matter where they happen, are a commitment which says, "For this time, I am concentrating on knowing you."

Discomfort in social settings should be no surprise. A principle of organic chemistry is: Like mixes with like. Those reagents which have similar properties will mix readily in solution with each other. In the chem lab of life, like mixes readily with like too. Perhaps because time spent with people of similar interests is easy and fun, stepping out and seeking those unlike oneself in life-style is rare. Yet biblically, the banquet table is for all: the poor, the outcast, friends, neighbors, the sojourner.

Asking for the company of someone you think has no interest in you may seem awkward at first. The discussion may make you bite your tongue in disagreement, but you'll have been exposed to another walk of life, and, if you're wise, you'll try to live it with the person while you can. Take the chance to experience a person who may stretch you. A wise woman who is given to hospitality once remarked, "Those people that are completely unlike myself are those I choose for best friends. They are the ones I can learn from. If I wanted to spend time feeding on myself, then I'd seek out those of similar opinions to mine." She has chosen the route that forces her from her own experience. No wonder she is given to hospitality. She knows all types of people not just as guests but as friends.

Part 2

The Single Person and the Church

9

Singles in All Shapes and Sizes

Who is meant by the term *single adults?* Approximately one-third of American adults—about 47 million—are currently unmarried. Of these, 10 percent have never married. Most of them are in their early 20s. Women outnumber men, especially among those who've lost spouses to death.

In the first chapter, identity was defined as "I-am-ness." Single people are not all alike, and they have differing views and attitudes toward the single life they are living.

Few of life's statuses are quite so clear as singleness and marriage. A profession defines someone, but is not exclusive. Hobbies define people somewhat, and so do many other things. But, a part-time single doesn't exist, and no one is just picking up marriage as a hobby. Even though roles within the different statuses may vary greatly, the people in the world are either married or single.

Singleness and the Biblical Writers

Scripture doesn't say much about marriage or singleness. It just wasn't a topic of life-saving importance to the biblical writers. What is written has always caused at least some ripples because the statements made are often very dogmatic and seem contradictory. Proving anything from isolated readings of various parts of Scripture would be easy.

What are these infamous passages? 1 Corinthians 7 is no

doubt the most colorful and easy to remember. This is where Paul sometimes get his "antimarriage" image. The critical passages about single living read: "Yet I wish that all men were even as I myself am. However, each man has his own gift from God, one in this manner, and another in that. But I say to the unmarried and to widows that it is good for them if they remain even as I" (vv. 7-8). And: "But I want you to be free from concern. One who is unmarried is concerned about the things of the Lord, how he may please the Lord; but one who is married is concerned about the things of the world, how he may please his wife, and his interests are divided. And the woman who is unmarried, and the virgin, is concerned about the things of the Lord, that she may be holy both in body and spirit; but one who is married is concerned about the things of the world, how she may please her husband. And this I say for your own benefit; not to put a restraint upon you, but to promote what is seemly, and to secure undistracted devotion to the Lord" (vv. 32-35).

The rest of the 1 Corinthians 7 passage doesn't paint a lovely picture of marriage. In fact, it almost seems as though Paul went out of his way to make it look bad and the single life good. In the first seven verses and verses 10 through 16, Paul describes the discord and lack of peace that marriage often brings. He calls marriage a place for those without self-control (v. 9). He hints that marriage could mean slavery (v. 23).

In contrast to this, Paul speaks of marriage to the Ephesians (5:21-33) almost with reverence. He calls the mystery of marriage "great" (v. 32). He uses such words as love, nourish, cherish, glory, and respect. The husband and wife are to present themselves before God holy and blameless. He repeats the Genesis passage that established marriage: "For this cause a man shall leave his father and mother, and shall cleave to his wife; and the two shall become one flesh" (5:31; see Gen. 2:24).

Judging by the number of sermons on marriage based on Paul's words, calling Paul anti-marriage would be unfair. What might be concluded? That Paul really was a flighty character in his opinions?

1 Corinthians 7:17 offers a clue. Paul wrote, "Only, as the Lord has assigned to each one, as God has called each, in this manner let him walk. And thus I direct in all the churches."

A logical conclusion is that Paul believed in both states, knew that God did as well, and tried to paint a realistic picture.

Other passages in the Bible have a pattern similar to these two Pauline passages. Genesis 2:18 reads, "The Lord God said, 'It is not good for the man to be alone; I will make him a helper suitable for him.'" The helper wasn't another man, but a woman. God shows His grand basic design for marriage in these verses.

Jesus showed a remarkable understanding of the single and married callings. In response to the question on divorce, he reaffirmed God's intent in marriage saying, "'Have you not read, that He who created them from the beginning made them male and female, and said, "For this cause a man shall leave his father and mother, and shall cleave to his wife; and the two shall become one flesh"? Consequently they are no more two, but one flesh. What therefore God has joined together, let no man separate'" (Matt. 19:4-6).

Yet Jesus clearly supported the single life. He said, "'For there are eunuchs who were born that way from their mother's womb; and there are eunuchs who were made eunuchs by men; and there are also eunuchs who made themselves eunuchs for the sake of the kingdom of heaven. He who is able to accept this let him accept it'" (19:12).

The writer of the Proverbs, who regularly criticized any and all conditions of human life including marriage, wrote, "He who finds a wife finds a good thing, and obtains favor from the Lord" (Prov. 18:22).

These readings bring a certain sort of security. Obviously neither life-style is superior. Therefore, no one has to make a change to find approval from God or the church (at least, in theory).

Several things can be deduced. Paul, Jesus, and others made it clear that neither calling is easy. Neither brings unusual glory to the person who is in that position.

God wants both married and single people to honor *Him*. Neither marital state is extremely important in the long-range view and is only a way to live out a life of service. God wants our focus on *Him*, not on life's externals.

How Singles View Themselves

An exploration of the single life yields the discovery that not everyone views himself or herself the same way. This is important for the church, and especially pastors, to remember, since all singles, no matter how they view themselves, want attention from the church.

Singles' groups would seem like the answer to all the singles' discontent and the church's neglect. Many singles in the church don't want to be identified with those groups. Other singles socialize and meet their spiritual needs only with other singles.

Despite this difference in social patterns, singles meet their own needs in very similar ways. They have predominantly single friends (though maybe only one or two) and behave as do other singles. Still, they don't want to be recognized as "single." They most often say, "Treat me as a human, not as a single." This can be difficult for a sympathetic pastor who is seeking to minister to singles and is hearing cries in both directions—one asking for special attention, the other vociferously rejecting it.

Another way of identifying singles and their opinions of

themselves revolves around the prospect of marriage. Singles approach the prospect of marriage in their lives in four basic ways.

Some prefer marriage. However, these singles are basically happy the way they are, and are willing to live with the creative tension of leaving their options open while pursuing a full life. They accept today and the future for what it is and make long-range plans accordingly. As singles, they want to live the best single life they can.

These people's ministry often includes other singles. They have established gracious patterns for handling the struggles of the single life and continually accept the challenges each day. Therefore, they can really sympathize with those who have difficulty.

Some singles want to get married at any cost. They make their wishes no secret. Just ask them what they want. They want to get married and the sooner the better. These persons often value marriage more than the persons they are marrying. If they don't get married, they feel angry, bitter, misled, and a failure. Mark W. Lee, at the Continental Congress on the Family, said these people should form a "major issue" for the church since their marriages number the highest with marital difficulties.

Some singles wish to remain single. These are intelligent, happy, productive, loving people who accept their own sexuality and marital state. As might be suspected, they are usually involved in service, both to the church and its members and to their professions. The issue of singleness has long been settled and life now is a matter of fulfilling a calling. This may or may not be temporary. I knew one man who spent the first 10 years out of undergraduate school thoroughly believing that he was called to single living. In that 10th year, his desires changed. In the 11th year, so did his marital status. But for many years, he was more than content; he was happy.

Singles Outside the Church

Of special interest to me is not how the church views singles, or how singles within the church view themselves, but how singles outside the church view both.

Not long ago, a friend casually shared his observation of a pattern in which women and men returned to the church when they married, and most often to the denomination in which they were born. Why? Some say people always return to their roots, but why at marriage? The old line is that people settle down when they marry. But a lot of married people have never settled down, and a lot of marrieds were never stirred up. So marriage doessn't seem to mean going back to church.

Why then do so many people snore into their pillows every Sunday morning? The general mood of the unchurched public today is not antireligious. It's quite the opposite, though the turn toward religion represents a move not to repentance but a search for divine meaning in the cosmos. It's a spiritual type of hedonism and escapism.

Addressing the religious has been left largely to the para-church organizations, those specifically organized for evangelizing. But many singles' groups in the church seem to be halfway points for singles who don't go to church. Many singles' group leaders point to the large number of unchurched singles who attend their groups. The wholesome company and attention to the critical areas of life attract them. Many have become believers because of this, and these group leaders anticipate many more such stories.

Church often lacks appeal to those who are aggressively pursuing their goals. The church image of settledness and family is particularly unattractive to single men who want to identify more with the "Marlboro man" than with the local divinity student. This problem is unusually acute among those who are innovators. Today's typical church seems to resist change; it's locked in with a board of directors consisting of businessmen over the age of 50. Church leaders link minds and keep out those who would disrupt that which they've created, even if it would revitalize church life. So, the young people who "see visions," as the prophet Joel said, find elsewhere to exercise their ideas. They get more respect from their peers and business associates than from their church. The church would do well to remember that David began his conquests at a very early age, as did Solomon and Jesus Himself. Even corporations recognize young talent. Charles Percy, a United States senator from Illinois, was president of Bell and Howell at the age of 25.

Another criticism of the church is that it's not in touch with reality. The church often gives the impression it is still fighting the moral battles of years past. A thinking person doesn't want to be locked into a stagnating enclosure. The singles' group is a touch closer to the world of singles at large.

The church needs to view what is essential to truth and godly living and worship, and to see what is peripheral, unnecessary, or even only ceremonial. Shedding some of those things that are a barrier to those who might want to believe in Jesus Christ, but don't find the church at all appealing, wouldn't hurt.

10

The Household of God

Today's younger single is a product of the American Dream. Mother and Dad were "upwardly mobile," cutting out a life together, making payments on a house, sending him to the neighborhood schools. That American initiative is deeply ingrained. Even though denouncing money and the American way of life has been chic, the root value of the American dream—personal success at whatever goal is set—has been kept.

Quality of life must never be violated under the new dream of the "good life." The good life is meaningful work, good interpersonal relationships, growing as individuals, times of silence and retreat. Christians spend a lot of time and energy growing themselves: pruning, weeding, and basking in sunlight. Though they have not succumbed to esthetic and spiritual hedonism, personal gain is still the number-one goal.

Individuality and Corporateness

Recently, a Latin American couple addressed our church. They were asked to share what they thought the North American church could learn from its southern neighbors. They talked of community and being God's people, pointing out that Christianity's roots are not in individualism but in God speaking corporately to His people.

Throughout the Old Testament, God dealt with Israel as a

nation. The Old Testament story is not only one of individuals and each person's relationship to God, but of Israel's corporate relationship to God. Moses led the Israelites from Egypt. The account of Israel's travels through the wilderness repeatedly reveals God speaking to the whole nation. God delivered the Ten Commandments. He punished Israel for building the golden calf. He allowed thousands to be bitten by poisonous snakes, for which the only antitoxin was a look at an uplifted brazen serpent. He led the people in celebration when enemies were defeated.

Whole nations were judged by a righteous God and peoples were destroyed for evil deeds or spared graciously when they turned their eyes to God. The prophets spoke to whole nations as well as to rulers, foretelling the hope of the Messiah, but also speaking of the condemnation of the unrighteous.

Today God speaks to the body of Christ—that collection of individuals who are the kingdom on earth. The image of a King with a kingdom is a useful one for this age. The word "kingdom" implies a ruler and subjects. Christ is King, the Lord, and Christians are the servants of the King as individuals and as the body of Christ.

Christians are not only allowed to experience an intense love relationship with Christ but they also have the privilege and responsibility to fellowship and serve with other believers, to be that body of Christ, to be interdependent, to experience God's love, reward (and even chastisement) for His people. In short, to be subjects of the King. The Apostle Paul used aliens, but you are fellow-citizens with the saints, and are of an analogy to everyday living to describe this. He wrote to the Ephesians: "So then you are no longer strangers and God's household" (Eph. 2:19).

The image of a household is a much warmer and closer one to our daily existence than that of a kingdom. A household is made up of a group of individuals who live together either as an extended family or nuclear family. They have daily contact and care for one another. What one does affects another.

In this way individual believers are united with each other through salvation. Jesus' death on the cross united Christians both with Him and with each other as fellow-citizens of the Kingdom.

But, just as personal salvation and forgiveness of sin is not a license for evil, becoming the household of God is not a reason for neglecting the growing together as individuals. The Ephesian passage that so clearly states that believers have an irreversible relationship to each other, also expands on principles of growth. "So then you are no longer strangers and aliens, but you are fellow-citizens with the saints, and are of God's household, having been built upon the foundation of the apostles and prophets, Christ Jesus Himself being the cornerstone, in whom the whole building, being fitted together is growing into a holy temple in the Lord; in whom you also are being built together into a dwelling of God in the Spirit" (Eph. 2:19-22).

The church must constantly nurture the corporate relationship. Paul mixed his images in the above passage, but the words are active—"having been built," "being fitted together," "growing into a holy temple," "being built together."

The early church knew how important unity was. In the midst of persecutions, when Peter and John were jailed, Luke recorded that "the congregation of those who believed were of one heart and soul" (Acts 4:32).

Jesus knew what was to come. "Holy Father, keep them in Thy name, the name which Thou hast given Me, that they may be one, even as We are" (John 17:11). He requested "that they may all be one; even as Thou, Father, art in Me, and I in Thee, that they also may be in Us; that the world may believe that Thou didst send Me" (17:21). The church is a witness to the world of the unity of God the Father with God the Son. As Christians, single and married, young and old, professional and vocational, the church is to be a witness to that unity.

The corporateness of believers is fleshed out in the local church. What does it mean to be corporate, or unified? It does not mean bland homogeneity. Rather, the unity of the church is dynamic, and tolerant of the individuality of its members.

The Segmentation of the Household

Sunday School is divided into the young marrieds' class, the women's group, the men's prayer meeting, and, most recently, singles' groups. Social activities revolve around peers as well. For the most part, the church has spent more time developing individuals than a corporate identity.

Segmentation does separate, but this kind of separation breeds identity. People of common interests come together to find support. What segmentation doesn't do is foster understanding of those of differing positions and life-style.

At the other end of the spectrum is the church that allows for no diversity of its members, especially in theology. This is not unity but conformity. Unity implies the coming together of two parts, which may or may not lose their individual characteristics. Conformity requires the loss of individuality.

The Apostle Paul acknowledged the tension between unity and diversity, and instructed the church to become unified while fully accepting the diverse backgrounds of its members.

Therefore remember, that formerly you, the Gentiles in the flesh, who are called 'Uncircumcision' by the so-called 'Circumcision,' which is performed in the flesh by human hands—remember that you were at that time separate from Christ, excluded from the commonwealth of Israel, and strangers to the covenants of promise, having no hope and without God in the world. But now in Christ Jesus you who formerly were far off have been brought near by the blood of Christ. For He Himself is our peace, who made both groups into one, and broke down the barrier of the dividing wall, by abolishing in His flesh the enmity, which is the law of commandments contained in ordinances, that in Himself He might make the two into one new man, thus establishing peace, and might reconcile them both in one body to God through the cross, by having put to death the enmity (Eph. 2:11-16).

Paul understood the practical realities of believers living in unity. Barriers and particular sets of conflicting experiences do not vanish when people become Christians, nor should they. Paul expected Jews and Gentiles to overcome years of division because Christ was their peace. It was not just a matter of a different life-style; it involved ordinances, laws, principles central to Jewish and Gentile concepts of society.

Steps to Unity

Cannot Paul's talk of the differences between Jews and Gentiles be applied to the singles and marrieds of the church today?

The first step to unity is to realize diversity and to find out what our dividing walls are. Some of the most obvious are: family life vs. single life; parenting responsibilities vs. peer responsibilities; home-life entertainment vs. group and dating entertainment; husband/wife relationships vs. independence; and (for some women) homemaking vs. employment or career. None of these is intrinsically bad, and how small they seem in comparison to the barriers between the first century Jews and Gentiles. Yet, for the person who is hurting, for the one who doesn't fit, they are mountains.

The church is a married institution, though married people have never conspired to functionally exclude single people from the mainstream of church life. Emphasis on individuals necessarily means that the most common interests of the majority will dominate any church body. This seems logical and democratic, but it places the person or peoples with minority viewpoints, special needs, or unusual life-styles outside of the mainstream and forces them to take second place to the majority needs and programs.

Yet, emphasis on the individual is an important conceptual part of the household of God. The Apostle Paul spoke of the "body" in a passage that has become familiar to any observant churchgoer. "And He gave some as apostles, and some as prophets, and some as evangelists, and some as pastors and teachers, for the equipping of the saints for the work of service, to the building up of the body of Christ; until we all attain to the unity of the faith, and of the knowledge of the Son of God, to a mature man, to the measure of the stature which belongs to the fulness of Christ" (Eph. 4:11-13).

If a body of believers is to realize its purposes, it has to be supportive of the excitement of the nervous system as well as of the dirt work of the digestive tract. It has to be as supportive of the single person in an evangelistic ministry as it is of Sunday School.

Paul stated that unity with diversity will create certain characteristics in a group of believers, singles and marrieds. "As a result, we are no longer to be children, tossed here and there by waves, and carried about by every wind of doctrine, by the trickery of men, by craftiness in deceitful scheming; but speaking truth in love, we are to grow up in all aspects into Him, who is the head, even Christ, from whom the whole body, being fitted and held together by that which every joint supplies, according to the proper working of each individual part, causes the growth of the body for the building up of itself in love" (Eph. 4:14-16).

By adopting the concept of unity with diversity, Christians can become mature and protect themselves from deceit and trickery. They are to speak truth in love—truth about doctrine, about hurts and anger, about burdens, about needs, about missions—in order to "grow up in all aspects of Him."

Confronting another is painful. To withhold deep-felt needs and hurt is a mockery to the unity Christ came to establish. The church must decide *as a group* if it is to have "unity at any cost," which denies any kind of differences and stifles honest, and possibly hurtful, confrontation. Or, it must decide *as a group* if it is to have "unity that costs everything," the kind of unity in which love and acceptance overcomes even the most hurtful confrontations.

Love is the essential element of this unity; it is the steel in the tension wire. Paul admonished, "And beyond all these things put on love, which is the perfect bond of unity" (Col. 3:14).

Paul didn't make love a central issue in his letter to the Ephesians, but sprinkled the text with such phrases as: "for the building up of [the body] in love" (4:16), "forbearance to one another in love" (4:2), "rooted and grounded in love" (3:17), "walk in love, just as Christ also loved you" (5:2). None of the truths he talks of are possible without that love.

Loving is easy until the going gets rough. But it's when tempers are stretched, and values and things held dear are challenged, that true love shows or doesn't show.

In the church I attend, we have confronted each other in some difficult ways; one confrontation lasted for almost a year. One group said, "We believe we should try operating this way." The other group countered. "We disagree. We shouldn't operate that way but in another." The issue, the selection of women elders, was personal as well as doctrinal.

As the months went by, tempers rose and people took sides. The discussions were heated, not without raised voices, which always caused an emotional drain. A group of women, who had joined together to study women's issues, wrote a paper on the biblical and historical perspective on women in the church.

Yet in that time, each side started listening to the other. We had hurt each other, but out of that grew a new awareness of the value of the individual. We ended up agreeing to disagree. Our existence as a body was not dependent on agreeing, but it was dependent on love. It was not dependent on peace, though the result of months of fiery discussions and painful confrontation was peace.

Peace, then, comes as the result of love and acceptance of diversity and disagreement. Peace is not an outer tranquility like oil on water; it is an inner condition of love and acceptance. Where true love and acceptance reside, peace will most assuredly follow, "for He Himself is our peace, who made both groups into one, and broke down the barrier of the dividing wall" (Eph. 2:14).

Any love relationship can last only if those involved are willing to work at it. On entering the household of God on the day of your salvation, you are given the means to live peacefully and lovingly, through the love of God in Jesus Christ. That's not a lot of piety and self-righteousness. That's a solid, down-to-earth challenge to be the family of God. Are you willing "to (be) diligent to preserve the unity of the Spirit in the bond of peace"? (Eph. 4:3)

Then you must be willing to "speak the truth in love," lay aside the old self," "put on the new self," "lay aside falsehood," "be angry, and yet do not sin; do not let the sun go down on your anger," "be kind to one another, tenderhearted, forgiving each other, just as God in Christ also has forgiven you."

Risking yourself to love one another is tricky business. After all, you might get burned. But God wants His people to be one as a witness to the unity of the Father and the Son. That necessitates risk.

Put imagination to work to apply the following passage from Romans to the church today. "I urge you therefore, brethren, by the mercies of God, to present your bodies [today's church?] a living and holy sacrifice, acceptable to God, which is your spiritual service of worship. And do not be conformed to this world, but be transformed by the renewing of your mind, that you may prove what the will of God is, that which is good and acceptable and perfect" (Rom. 12:1-2).

11

Who's Knocking at the Church Door?

The purpose of the church is for believers to fellowship together. This is not fellowship of the coffee and cookie variety, but the serious business of being the body of Christ, since theoretically, all the other business of being the church could be accomplished alone. In discussing the purpose of the local church David Mains observed: "Conceivably, local churches could be eliminated were it not for the great need Christians have to discuss their faith with one another" (*Full Circle,* Waco, Tex.: Word, 1971, p. 48). Christians need each other to grow in Christ, for support, for rebuke, for love, for teaching.

In fellowship in the church, people mold people. Groups mold people. The positive aspect of this is called discipleship, conforming to the image of Christ. Indeed, this is, or should be, every Christian's personal goal. Along with the good, though, comes the unnecessary. Conforming to peers places stress on individual expression, because people are reluctant to be different from one another. Fellowshiping includes the unvoiced expectation that the individual will reach out to the group and not necessarily expect the group to return the effort. This is why women don't visit the men's prayer group, why men don't attend bridal showers, and why a non-Christian changes the tone of a Bible study. Groupness is lost when those with unchangeable traits attend and participate.

The continual emphasis on married and family life in fellowship unconsciously invalidates the life of the single. In order to be part of most churches, single persons must continually filter all that goes on, gleaning that which applies to them. Or they must get married.

Both single and married people share responsibility for the institutional assumptions and practices that leave single people out of church life and the church out of the lives of too many single Christians. Both single and married people need to understand the attitudes of each other and of church leaders who contribute to the problem, not to pass judgment on their brothers and sisters but to be able to cope and correct and to help the whole church grow in this area.

The Response of the Single

Singles usually respond in two ways if they don't get married: they leave the local church, or they accept the conditions and remain. Those who leave seek an atmosphere where they are accepted and can achieve a sense of groupness, if they continue their interest in the church at all. Churches with singles' ministries attract many who haven't found acceptance elsewhere.

Those who accept the conditions and remain are valiant indeed. The single person who remains with his or her local church can be numbered with the faithful, because more initiative and sacrifice is required to identify primarily with those whose life-style is different from one's own. Just how many times have missionaries, who've chosen to exclusively identify with nationals for all their needs, found this to be true?

Some will argue that this whole presentation is hypersensitive. No one is barred from the pew. Church people are all civil. And don't they pray for each other and support each others' needs? Are not the major issues of the Christian life unrelated to marriage or singleness? Effective prayer, Bible study, evangelism, and servanthood touch all humans in amazingly similar ways, over all ages, over all life-styles. The message of Christ is universal. The basic needs of all humans are universal as well. Concluding that those who perceive these hurts are feeling unrealistically sorry for themselves may be logical. Hurts, disappointments, and a feeling of being left out are the conditions of many marrieds as well and are common to the general human condition.

Viewed from the minority position, however, these hurts are not the same as general human hurts. They are institutional, the result of the church's current life-style.

In general, the church as an institution seems to have decided how it will meet needs. Not only are the needs ranked in importance, but some needs are not even thought of as being important. In one sense, the church has legislated on the validity of complaints and hurts, and has turned its back on the ones it creates.

One of the hurts many singles feel is rejection because they aren't married. And many singles, in an effort to be acceptable, run a neurotic race to the altar. Catch your loved one quick before the good ones are gone, and the pickings become slim. The question "Why aren't you married?" with its implied meaning, "You're going to be left out if you aren't," becomes a source of irritation.

The Apostle Paul strongly suggested that those who can remain unmarried should do so (1 Cor. 7). He called single living the highest life-style. Many take this rather lightly. In fact, calling singleness a gift of God makes them recoil. If they get the gift, they'll try to return the package to the sender unopened. And tagging single living the "highest" of life-styles seems, at best, naive of Paul; at worst, a cruel joke.

As if this dilemma isn't enough, the church often doesn't see its own responsibility in the matter. The single's problems are unseen as singles' problems. Neither married church men and women nor singles see the cause and effect relationship.

If asked to take their share of responsibility for the single person's discomfort, it's doubtful that married people could see it. They end up blaming the victim (the single) for his or her problem. Singles are asked to bear the burden of singleness alone. In *Body Life* (Glendale, California: Regal, 1972), Ray C. Stedman lists the five works of the ministry, one of which is "to set at liberty the oppressed" (Luke 4:18; Isa. 61:1). Does oppression cause the body of Christ to deny one of the gifts of God? Does the emphasis on married life cause the single to live in bondage?

The Church's Response

The church needs to review itself in order to determine its part in creating bondage for single adults. By nature, this process will be difficult because the disease is systemic, infecting almost every attitude and event. The sin is institutional, and therefore, the cure cannot be effected by cutting out the diseased part. Church life-style, on every level, must be altered to include all those deviant to the norm. On the practical level, that means closer attention to all those activities and programs sponsored by the church. No small task.

A number of things become obvious when thinking of where the church needs to review itself:

Adult education should include all adults and not unnecessarily segment the local church body. Sunday School classes are often divided into the young marrieds, the old marrieds, the senior citizens, the career group, and what have you. Though these divisions are superficial and hinder the free flow of adult interaction, they are not always discriminatory or unfair. They usually divide along two needs: to identify with opinions and to diversify among opinions.

A group identifying with opinions convenes for the purpose of exploring a common problem or aspect of their lives. A group of homemakers might get together to learn how to evangelize their neighbors through neighborhood Bible studies. Singles might get together to discuss their own needs in relationship to the church. A special interest group could decide to report to the congregation on what they learned or accomplished as a way of keeping the body in touch. These groups could also submit recommendations for change within the church. Important to these groups is that they have a point of termination. Unless the group ends, it becomes exclusive, keeping others from entering the fellowship.

For a group with diversity of opinions, the aim is to collect a variety of individuals who have different opinions on the topic discussed. This type of study can be about almost anything, from basic Bible study to issues of church structure to contemporary world affairs. In colorful dialogue, people grow and adjust their opinions, or convince others that they're right.

The reason for keeping people flowing from group to group is obvious. Only by constant interaction can the church's people ever achieve awareness of each other and others' points of growth.

Nowhere in society but the church are people segmented to such a great extent. Work brings all types of people together. Families have all ages. But in the church, the temptation is to classify. To remain fresh and new and mobile requires effort. In the case of adult education, standing is moving backward, both in content of material and in the exchange of opinions.

Breaking down discriminatory traditions requires constant attention to the methods and words in which content is presented. Announcements, church bulletins, sermons, even hymns need to be screened for their content in terms of offensive or exclusive words, phrases, and analogies. In particular, analogies to marriage and family life have to be balanced with examples from single life. "You and your family will want . . ." might be changed to "Everyone, singles and families, will want . . ." "In your homes" may be reworded as "In your homes or apartments." "Women, after the children have gone to school, you might . . ." should begin, "Mothers, . . ." for not all women are mothers. Wherever a group is addressed, care should be taken to distinguish between those not addressed by the message.

This kind of effort may seem bothersome and superficial, but reeducating a group of people calls for a persistent effort on every level. Symbolic and token gestures are essential. Both attitudes and actions need adjusting. The problem must always be up front. Draft card burning, civil rights marches, and bra burning as acts did little for their respective movements. They were symbols for what these social activists actually wanted. Their value was in drawing attention to the problems.

The reason for all this hoopla is that institutions and traditions are slow to change, even when they have destructive qualities. The traditional method for handling groups outside the mainstream of the church is to form a subgroup. Thus singles' groups, senior citizens' groups, women's circles, and youth groups. These groups have limited value. Most of their value resides in being something with which people can identify. The problem is that often they ghettoize. Senior citizens' groups become hobby clubs. Women's groups become social or service project oriented. Youth groups become weak surrogates for the family. Singles' groups become adult nursery schools. Escape from these groups seems impossible. The goal of any side group should be to become obsolete, directing people to the heterogeneous fellowship of the whole church, or at least to be constantly evolving, directing the participants to bigger and better things.

Singles' groups, in order to be effective, must have unmarried leaders, be a recognized part of the church, and be grass roots in origin. Singles have an incredible amount of energy and a wealth of creativity that is all too often untapped. Preconceived notions about their lack of maturity and importance in the church keep them from fleshing out the talent that is there. A married church, with married ways, usually doesn't meet the needs singles have for social involvement and identity. Singles' groups are valid for those reasons, but other goals are equally, if not more, valuable than these two.

For their own self-respect and that of the group, the leaders of any singles' group should be unmarried. In fact, if at all possible, no married person should have anything to do with leadership. Nevertheless, some married people have unique gifts, insights, and commitment that allow them a role in ministry with singles, often as an advocate and ally of single perspectives to married church leaders. Of course, all of the recognized groups of a church will be directly or indirectly under the leadership of the church, but no special leadership should be put in the direction of singles. Singles' retreats especially should *not* have married leadership, and if at all possible, avoid married speakers. This is a simple principle, yet it's the one that appears to be the most violated. At one of our church's singles' retreats, our women shared a cabin with women from another retreat. Lights had to be out at 11 P.M. It seemed incredible that adults, all over 22, couldn't be trusted to put themselves to bed.

Singles' groups should be recognized as a part of the church and be held accountable for growth and input to the church. The charge of immaturity has been leveled too often. The lack of heavy singles participation in the church was another root cause. Singles as a group have had low expectations and a low self-image, so ingrained is the idea that adulthood begins with marriage. With the recognition of value and stated expectations, singles' groups will become a viable part of church life. This will take continual reminders from the pulpit and active recruitment of singles to leadership and decision-making roles.

Any singles' group should be grass roots in origin. Singles need to recognize their own needs and act on them without a push from others. Whoever begins the group will by default become the leader. In original movements, no democratic elections can possibly take place, so that is the fate of the originator. Obviously, then, this is why that person should be single; so that leadership from the very start is indigenous. All leadership, direction, and planning should be solely in the hands of the unmarried.

It is important for the singles of the church to "own" their own group. The victories, defeats, and lessons belong to those who tried to make it work. When a person becomes involved, everything that occurs happens to something they've had a part in creating. Investing part of oneself virtually insures commitment and a sense of belonging. This is a position of security from which leadership can grow.

In the last analysis, singles' groups should self-destruct. Their value is very limited, and always self-centered. Gaining an identity has value in itself, but once that's done, they need to move on to more other-centered activities. If a group is fluid, with many people moving in and out, then perhaps instead of disbanding, the group leaders should continually see where they can plug participants into other areas of the church. This could mean two-group involvement for individuals, with the singles and another group, which probably would be easily accomplished.

Both singles and the church should recognize leadership gifts within singles and work toward developing those gifts. Leadership structures vary so much between churches that almost no generalizations about singles in leadership can be made. Church leadership in a small church usually amounts to a pastor and spouse. Huge churches, in contrast, have a complex leadership structure of boards, committees, study groups, prayer groups, and fellowships.

Leadership positions, with hardly any thought to the contrary, are awarded to the married. A few reasons for this are obvious. One is that leadership positions are most often given to the older members of the congregation, and the older the parishioner, the more likely he or she is to be married. Another reason is that since the church generally attracts more marrieds than singles, more marrieds will assume leadership.

Are there so many more married adults in the church that there is no single leadership? Is the lack of single leadership the reason so many singles stay away from the church? My guess is that it is both. Yet, the more glaring piece of evidence is that older singles don't participate in leadership either. Some of these singles have logged thousands of hours in church work too. The erroneous assumptions of both marrieds and singles are that married people are mature, single people are immature, and that married people will be stable and singles transient, are difficult to escape. Like many other assumptions, these are generally unvoiced, but nevertheless a force in the outworkings as the body of Christ.

This is no reason for a congregation to make a 25-year-old medical student chairman of the board, but there is reason to look at that single person as potential leadership. This leadership is the leadership presented in Philippians 2 and the Isaiah servant poems. The leader is first and foremost a servant of the people and of God. Developing godly leadership is more a matter of learning servanthood than anything else. With this in mind, servant/leaders can be in training at any age, and can assume leadership at almost any age.

As the one who sets the tone and pace of the church, the pastor must continually promote the health and wholeness of the church, both individually and corporately. The position of pastor is powerful. Church life gains its impetus and mood from the pastor's personality.

Few pastors are unmarried, mainly because churches usually don't want unmarried pastors. They don't believe that an unmarried person could reach families.

Then can married pastors minister to singles? Yes, they can. Wisdom can be imparted to most anyone for the asking. What we see today is that not many married pastors know how to minister to singles. One pastor once told me that "single women who are professionals obviously have the gift of singleness because they don't have an interest in home life and don't need men to take care of them." This promotes the stereotype of the cold, insensitive, masculine, working single woman. A Christian education director once took it upon himself to minister to the older single males "because they always have such difficult and deep-rooted problems." It's nice that older, single males are getting some attention, but shouldn't it be a little less like psychiatric treatment? The assumption is that any man could be married and there must be something wrong if he isn't.

The pastor's heavy emphasis on using sermon illustrations based on marriage and family life has already been mentioned. But that is not the core. The philosophy presented each Sunday comes from someone whose life experience is predominantly married. Nothing will change this. The best a pastor can do is to continually be in contact with the single adults in his church. Indeed, the pastor should try to live their experiences vicariously.

This sounds like a lot of effort for someone whose workload is already great. But single people have for years adapted all kinds of messages to their lives. A sensitive minister will want to reach to every corner of the congregation and adapt messages to include all.

Some suggestions. Always include relevant ties to other life-styles represented in the congregation when preaching on a special topic—Mother's Day, etc. (Please, no excuses that most singles will be married some day so the message is relevant.) Vary analogies as was mentioned before. Include singles in the worship service activities. From the pulpit, admonish single adults to live full and mature lives. Encourage all members to live as servants to one another.

In conclusion, society is already fragmented. The church needn't be as well. Through Jesus Christ, the church has the power to be a source of healing, restoration, and dynamic living to all those who would receive Him. Allowing something as superficial as marital status to keep the church from experiencing the totality of the Father's union with the Son is tragic.

12

Gifts, Goals, and Leadership

"You are gifted." It was the first time I had ever heard it stated so emphatically. The words rang in my ears and I became excited. *"You* are gifted." Again and again, David Mains would throw those words into his sermons to Circle Church. After a few months of hearing it, I began to believe: *I am gifted.*

I remembered having heard a talk on spiritual gifts when I was in college. The speaker emphasized then that all Christians possess at least one gift of the Holy Spirit. For one week after, I read everything I could and prayed, looked in me, around me, behind me, and still couldn't find any spiritual gift, much less more than one. Someone told me not to worry. That spiritual gifts usually meant speaking in tongues and that was something Pentecostals did. That was as much as I heard until I came back to Chicago and started going to a non-Pentecostal church that thrived on spiritual gifts.

In those first few months at Circle Church, I saw the Holy Spirit in action, empowering people in all kinds of ways and *creating,* something I thought had ended when God said it was "very, very good." It was the first truly positive approach to the spiritual experience I'd ever heard. So often what comes from the pulpit is "shape up." To hear the question, "What are your spiritual gifts and how are you going to use them?" was different. The result was a people who dared new things, and did the old and expected with a flair only the Holy Spirit can bring.

Gifts of the Holy Spirit

The gifts of the Holy Spirit and their manifestations are varied, but they have a common basis.

The gifts of the Holy Spirit are supernatural. Some of the gifts, such as healing, are miraculous. Others, such as service, music, or administration, use well-understood human means of operation. But they are all supernatural, empowered by the Holy Spirit. This empowering makes a preacher's sermon ring with truth, makes music another voice of God in spiritual service, gives strength and healing to a nurse's hand. For example, the nurses' duties will be the same for all nurses, but the nurse empowered by the Spirit will bring a healing that no medicine can.

Some believe that the gifts of the Spirit are limited to the 20 or more listed in Scripture. Another definition allows for anything done with spiritual empowering to be a gift, as long as the body of Christ is edified. Thus, talents can become gifts of the Spirit. This and many other debates among Christians about the Holy Spirit and His gifts are beyond the intent of this book. What is important is that spiritual gifts are the avenue of ministry in the church, and singles have gifts with which to serve.

The gifts of the Holy Spirit are for the common good. Paul wrote, "But to each one is given the manifestation of the Spirit for the common good" (1 Cor. 12:7). Peter concurred with this, urging believers to "employ (the gifts of the Spirit) serving one another" (1 Peter 4:10). God's gifts are for the edification of the body of Christ and when not employed for those uses cannot rightly be called gifts of the Spirit. In no instance of Scripture do we see a gift of the Spirit being used for any other reason than building the church.

Everyone possesses at least one gift of the Holy Spirit. In every mention of gifts the New Testament is exceedingly clear that *all* believers have at least one gift, indeed, most likely more than one. These gifts are complementary, as can be seen from the 1 Corinthians passage. Some are less showy than others, but none is less important than the others or contributes less to the well-being of the church.

Each Christian is to use the gifts given him or her by the Holy Spirit. Believers are called to an active empowering of the Holy Spirit. God wants a dynamic church. Paul wrote, "And since we have gifts that differ according to the grace given to us, let each exercise them accordingly (Rom. 12:6). Harmony and music of the soul rises from the congregation that freely meshes its gifts. Creativity and the lightening of burdens also result from the use of gifts. Burdens that are borne by those who have recognized their gifts don't necessarily become easier, but they are empowered.

God is not just a benevolent grandfather who gives treats to His grandchildren to see the smiles on their faces. Matthew 25 tells of the servants whose master had given them talents to use and multiply in value while the master was away. Two were faithful. The third hid his talent, bringing upon himself the wrath of the master when he returned. God likewise gives His gifts not just for fun and games but for the serious business of the kingdom.

The warning given in Matthew 25 can evoke two possible reactions. One is to get busy and use the gifts often. The other is to shy away from the gifts for fear of becoming "proud" or losing the centrality of Christ.

When spiritual gifts are recognized as a manifestation of the Holy Spirit, the person who is the vehicle of a gift will most likely be in reverent, jubilant awe of God. He will know the source of his gift. And the body of Christ with whom this gift is shared will know too, and should rejoice.

Why do some Christians hesitate to use a gift? One reason is a feeling of "I can't believe that God would entrust me with anything good." A second reason might be not wanting to appear to be more spiritual than those believers who haven't isolated their gifts. If no one steps forward with a gift, then no one is left out. Another inhibitor to the discovery of gifts is the lack of good role models. People just aren't using the gifts except for the more common ones or showy ones. I've been in a roomful of people who all believe their gifts are administration or service. That would be like saying the body is composed of only livers and left arms.

Not knowing how to discover the gifts is another inhibitor. When I first wanted to know mine, someone said, "Look at what you've already done." That only confused me more, because I've always been an all-points person. Either I had a dozen gifts, none of which were very well developed, or I had to choose from a field which wasn't very well defined. This method seems to have worked well for some, but not for me.

One way to isolate your gifts is to look at the desires of your heart. Christians are accustomed to thinking that what they like to do must be the opposite of what God wants them to do. But adults whose hearts are continually being renewed by the love of Christ should begin to trust their feelings of wanting to serve the Lord in a particular area.

Many people have wanted to write. But no writer was ever able to discover the gift without first sitting at a typewriter or picking up a pen and paper. You may like to write, but that's not the same as acting on a heartfelt desire and seeing how the Holy Spirit moves within that work. All reform and creativity have their cornerstones in an idea, whether human or planted by the Holy Spirit. The prophet Joel knew of the empowering of the Holy Spirit and foretold, "Your old men will dream dreams, your young men will see visions" (Joel 2:28).

Goals

All people have dreams, goals, or visions. They look to the

future and picture themselves at some place other than where they are now. Dreaming is pleasant. Surely the Apostles were visionaries. They must have imagined a world or at least a church with Christ as its head. Certainly Paul did. Paul expressed visions for high quality Christian living in the Books of Romans, Ephesians, and Galatians. He was continually moving toward a mark, and he expected the believers he addressed to move toward those same goals.

Goals become a touchy area for Christians. They are supposed to have no thought for personal aggrandizement, yet doing work well is an admonition for the laborer. But, having goals is more than working well; it is moving up on the ladder to success, however, it is defined. Christians have added another meaning to the definition of goals to include spiritual goals, as well as personal and professional goals. Oddly, the spiritual goals, which are strangest to the world at large, are frequently the most acceptable and respected in Christian circles.

Singles often put aside goals, especially career goals, until one specific goal—marriage—is accomplished. One counselor observed, "The main occupation for singles it seems is to see that each other gets married." How true. In some ways, though, marriage facilitates professional goals, especially for men who often almost *need* wives in order for management to take them seriously, or, in the case of seminarians, for most churches even to consider them seriously for pastoral spots.

Goals have a different meaning for single women than single men. Men expect to continue with their goals without breaks throughout their lives. Often, women will struggle with career vs. home life. This is changing, though, and more women are learning how to juggle motherhood with professional goals effectively. For the single woman, the struggle is not on that level. She doesn't know if she'll marry. So, pursuing a career becomes at least somewhat necessary, even if just to keep food on the table and the rent paid. The question of career is more complex than that, however. Statistically, the more educated the woman, the less likely it is that she'll marry. Men tend to marry down on the educational level and women usually marry up. This is a real dilemma for the gifted, educated woman who, beyond all else, really wants to get married.

So a woman might settle on a career that is less challenging than her talents call for. Or, she might postpone any career plans in order to be continually free to marry. This could be a goal-ignoring catastrophe. After 20 years of waiting for Prince Charming, Cinderella finally gives up and has made a pumpkin out of her life so far.

Incidents like these make one question the validity of marriage as a goal, especially since women face difficult odds —there are more women than men in the world. Another reason to question marriage as a goal is the very nature of marriage itself. Marriage is a way of life, not an arena for performance. It acts as a facilitator to life, not the main focus. Yet, marriage is traditionally a woman's most desirable *goal*. No wonder so many wives find their lives empty after the children have gone. The role of wife and mother is a busy one, but it's limited. As a primary occupation in life, being a wife and mother can fall short. At least, not *every* woman should be forced to see it as *her* major goal.

Another area related to goals is leadership. Thinking of leaders prompts a variety of images: Moses coming down from the mountain, Paul rejoicing in prison, Deborah (the Old Testament judge) leading Israel into battle. In today's terms it might be the president or a civil rights activist. Single people are rarely seen leading in relationship to the people around them, especially in the church. Interestingly enough, both Jesus and Paul were single, and Jesus started showing His leadership skills at the tender age of 12 by astounding the elders in the temple (Luke 2).

Singles as Leaders

Many singles don't think of themselves as leaders, and neither do the leaders in the church. In a discussion on church leadership at a retreat, the question was posed to a group of 20 single adults, all active church members, "Are we not involved in church leadership because we don't see ourselves as leaders?" This group, composed largely of young professionals, slowly nodded their heads in affirmation, and a few said Yes. They didn't envision themselves as church leaders even though most of them were assuming more and more job responsibility.

At the Continental Congress on the Family, Mark W. Lee argued for the placing of more responsibility in the hands of singles. "We let unmarried women become church secretaries or teachers of small children in Sunday School, and unmarried men become ushers. But why should they not become chairpersons of church boards, development officers, and the like? Singles may engage in Christian occupation and avocation without concern for the needs and comforts of mates. Unmarried Christian men and women appear to devote more time to their jobs and assignments than marrieds, are less concerned with financial rewards or recognition, and are more willing to do onerous chores. At the very least, singles should be identified equally with marrieds in the communion of the church" (Gary Collins, ed., *It's OK to be Single: A Guidebook for Singles and the Church*, Waco, Texas: Word, 1976, p. 51).

Singles have reputations for being transients and immature —almost entirely hearsay and preconceived notions. When quizzed as to why this was, one pastor suggested that the church never gets down to the "practical realities" of these viewpoints.

Parachurch organizations, often defined as evangelistic or ministering arms of the church, sometimes provide more outlets for the talents of singles than does the church itself. These organizations are not as concerned about old-age maturity as about getting the job done. So expressing creativity has promise.

A single man usually has good chances for advancement. A male in a parachurch organization usually doesn't remain single long, so great are the odds in favor of marriage just by the sheer numbers of unattached females.

For women, the story is quite different, though it is changing now. Single women almost always had to stick with low-responsibility jobs, with lower pay than their male counterparts (in the same positions who very quickly were promoted), as assistants to some executive. Some single women have hung on. When the organization is sure she won't marry and that she is a "lifer," she might get promoted. Men don't have to face the question, "Are you getting married soon?" when applying.

The mission field traditionally has been the place where single women go if they want to use their talents. As for men, mission boards usually prefer to send out men who are already married. In fact, single women who go overseas are often expected to stay single.

Missions, whether domestic or foreign, still remain as one of the most vital ways to serve God. Every ounce of effort in every area of service has to be expressed to get the job done. The work is hard, the pay exceptionally low, but the personal satisfaction at times is unparalleled by any kind of service in the United States.

Decision-making

The key to leadership is the ability to make good decisions. Decisions affect not only the course of your present and future life, but also the attitudes you have toward yourself.

Decision-making is always the means to an end. Without it, no change is ever made.

For Christians, decision-making is more complex because they are not relying on wits alone. Jesus is Lord of the Christian's life and that has significant meaning in the process of decision-making. Indeed, the Lordship of Christ should be the basis on which all decisions are made. The boundary between making Jesus Lord and abrogating all responsibility in the decision-making process is a fine line.

God is a thinking God. The very first sentence in the Bible is, "In the beginning, God created the heavens and the earth" (Gen. 1:1). The heavens and the earth are the product of God's thought. The first chapter of Genesis then details more of God's creative thought, always telling the reader that "it was good."

The precedence for human decision-making comes in Genesis 2:19, "And out of the ground the Lord God formed every beast of the field and every bird of the sky, and brought them to the man to see what he would call them; and whatever the man called a living creature, that was its name." Decision-making, then, is part of the image of God. God, in His relationship with the first human, encouraged decision-making. God did not say "this is what you will call the beasts." Rather, the decision was in the hands of the newly created man. Some might object, "Well, that was before the fall." This is true. But even the fall of Adam and Eve didn't change the fact that they and their descendants were created in God's image, and that creativity and thinking are remnants of that once perfect image.

Something about decision-making seems to be inherently "unspiritual." Perhaps it implies that one doesn't rely on God, or Jesus as Lord. It's as if the way to approach decisions were on a continuum. At one end are praying and listening to the Holy Spirit for direction. At the other end lies making the decision with no help from God at all. Varying degrees of either approach lie in between. The closer one gets to the first one, relying on the Holy Spirit, the more mature he or she is assumed to be.

Often we hear of those who have "stepped out on faith," only to have the prayer for the miraculous fall on its face, leaving the person disillusioned or at least wondering what went wrong. The conclusion is that God didn't will it, which undoubtedly has at least some truth to it. Various other reasons are given for why prayers haven't been answered, from the obvious to those that involve a great deal of mental gymnastics. For those who have miraculous answers to prayer, it is obvious who is behind them. And rejoicing is no difficulty.

When I think of decisions based solely on discerning the will of God, I imagine someone standing at the side of a frozen lake. He sees the other side and wants to get over there but has no idea of how thick the ice is and if it will support his body weight. He decides to run away.

Another model for decision-making for the Christian might include (1) listening to the Holy Spirit and decision-making as complements rather than antagonists and (2) many steps to deciding what the outcome of the situation should be. Too often it is assumed that reason and the will of God have nothing to do with each other.

Indeed, the need to make a decision should probably be prompted by the Holy Spirit. At some point, God says, "I want you to change." At other times, things might be so unproductive that change becomes the only way out. A person may have few friends because of excessive shyness and would need to overcome the shyness to make the friends he or she wants. Someone may feel that God has given him or her leadership abilities, but as yet they are still raw and unformed. The situations are endless. But they all have answers to three basic questions: Where are you? Where would you like/want to be? How are you going to get there?

You already know where you are. Next, select a goal—

where you want to be. It should be something both attainable and having observable results. Setting a goal of "reaching spiritual maturity" has inherent difficulties. First, you really don't know what you're aiming at. It is so vague and hard to define that you really won't know when you've achieved it. Second, the process is much too involved for one simple step, or even a few complicated ones. Third, you'll most likely never attain it, which would only be frustrating. An example of a more realistic goal might be: learning to be comfortable speaking before large or small audiences. You know what you're aiming at, you'll know when you've achieved it, and steps will be at least somewhat obvious on the way.

Next, as best as you can, isolate why you haven't as yet achieved this. Maybe you've never tried. On the other hand, you may have tried this many, many times and failed repeatedly. Knowing why you've failed is only a first step. The biggest step is believing that you *can* do what you want, without failing. Tackling an area of failure takes all the encouragement in the world, but God will help you.

Some have other reasons for not having achieved their goals in the past. They may have been brought up to believe they were incompetent. Most of the time, though, the goal is new because it is a new phase of life—buying a car, renting an apartment, deciding on a college major, or learning to cook.

The best thing about failures is that they are lessons for the future. If nothing else, they teach what *not* to do. They can serve to make you a bit wiser and the future more enjoyable.

How will you reach your goal? This involves the work. God is only too willing to listen to prayers, especially when it comes to tackling difficult areas of discipleship. Throughout the Psalms the writers even described God by His willingness to hear: "O Thou who dost hear prayer . . ." (Ps. 65:2). Grinding out the answers and making significant changes will take more than one prayer and one day. It will take many days and many small prayers. For example, because you want to overcome your shyness, you decide to read up on the different kinds of counseling available for the shy person. Assertiveness training looks pretty good, and you sign up. Throughout the course you ask God to make apparent those things He specifically wants you to learn about your shyness.

In the above example, prayer and action went hand in hand. The growth from the situation was dependent on both items, not only the prayer or the action. Too often Christians assume that new creation in Jesus Christ will happen in their sleep, that it will be effortless.

If you're shy, you might, after learning more about your shyness, decide the first step to take would be to say "hello" to people first, even strangers. You would pray for strength and the ability to accept any failures, plus give praise to God for His interest in solving the shy person's problem. This step involves some very real risks. You may find that some people won't respond to your "hello."

Risks and Decision-making

Risks go hand-in-hand with growth. In an analysis of risk, one psychologist set up a situation to see how people approached risk. Allowing the subjects to stand anywhere they wanted to, he asked them to throw a small rubber ball into a bucket. Some stood beside the bucket and more or less dropped the ball in. Others stood very far away and almost always missed. Most stood at a distance that was slightly challenging to their throwing ability.

He hypothesized that these people followed the same patterns in their decision-making processes in real life situations. Those who stood very near the bucket didn't get involved in situations where they could fail. They always took the low-risk way out, either by not attempting anything or doing only those things familiar to them. Those who stood far away were the gambler sort, always trying for the long shot. They failed often but risked big. Even with repeated failure, they kept trying things with a lot of risk. Those in the middle took calculated risks. They most likely chose to be moderately challenged in their daily lives.

The problem with risk is that it might mean failure, failure might mean hurt, and hurt might make you feel bad about yourself and keep you from risking again. Any growth situation has risk; without it nothing difficult is tried. So growing people are continually setting themselves up for the potential to be hurt.

Also, failure is not just having tried something and failed. It is often a way of life. The person who thinks he is a failure will carry that attitude into everything he tries. That person thoroughly believes, even if only subconsciously, that everything will somehow go sour. He approaches any situation—a job, a new love interest, woodworking—programmed to fail, not out of logical conclusions about intelligence or talent, but with subconscious conviction that this is his destiny. Such a person is caught up in self-fulfilling prophecy.

The Final Analysis

The great inhibitor to growth is indecision. Most people would rather have perplexing things behind them, which means either ignoring problems or making choices. Indecision can be a way of life too, just like failure. A person may cry, "Tell me what to do" about whether to take a job, where to move, whether to marry, or even what clothes to buy. People in restaurants who ask, "What are you having?" are looking for a clue as to what they should order.

The main difference between singles and marrieds is not

that they are different, but that the single person's lack of decision is recognized as such. Even the "decision to marry" may be a common myth. Given the social pressure to marry, marriage may be just a series of nondecisions. A relationship starts and one stage flows to the next. Before long the couple can find themselves married without ever having made a conscious decision to marry or even to select their spouse. Many singles, on the other hand, have consciously chosen not to be swept into weak marriages by chance.

One of the unfortunate characteristics of indecision is that it *is* a decision. The person has decided to postpone any of the benefits or mistakes of coming to a conclusion. It is a loss no matter what way you look at it, especially concerning large matters. Yet, people will go for years without tackling a needed decision. Single women postpone career plans waiting to get married. If they do marry, fine. If not, then careers may be started 20 years after they should have been. Very bright scholars sometimes will excel in their graduate studies but never attempt to develop relationships with anyone besides their books and will remain without friends for years.

Single people are often content to ride the waves of seemingly uncontrollable happenings, to accept nagging suspicions that they're not capable of those things that are difficult, or to write off failures and successes to "the will of God" and thereby avoid responsibility or the need to change.

Everyone has to be willing to risk and make life-changing decisions. No matter how much the Holy Spirit prods or how rotten life gets, nothing will change as long as you don't want it to and don't make the effort. God cannot mold your life unless you are willing to take steps.

13

The Newly Single

Neither divorce nor widowhood is new to the church. But the church is beginning to talk about the formerly married. It's making efforts to accept responsibility for the multitude of needs the widowed and divorced have.

For the widowed, one life-style ends and another has to take its place. Divorce is *completely* new to the single adult who closed the door on his or her marriage. Most Christians take marriage vows seriously, almost as seriously as their commitment to Christ, and never plan to divorce. Then if divorce occurs, it is accompanied by guilt, hurt, and bewilderment.

The Problems of the New Single

The newly singled person has many of the same concerns that "old timer" singles do. But these concerns are new to most of them, and the problems have a little something extra.

They are alone again. After years of having someone around, they have to make special effort to be with a companion. They wonder, "What do I do with a weekend?" because they haven't had to decide for years. Dating seems almost juvenile but it's a must if they want to meet anyone new or have entertainment. They are also "virgins" again, and for some, the adjustment to celibacy takes a long time.

At the loss of a spouse a sense of alienation pervades the

new single's consciousness because their own world has just been shattered, and they haven't yet made the transition to a new one. Social calendars changed, and they have to make their own friends. Like all singles, though, the newly singled person experiences the same feeling of being out of the mainstream of church—a church geared to the needs and concerns of the married population.

Formerly marrieds want to be treated as any other adult, not as objects of pity or ostracism. The church may disapprove of divorce, but it should not condemn the divorced person. Healing love needs to be freely extended to everyone, not on the basis of severity of sin. Divorced people have as many talents and gifts as they did before the divorce, and need to be put into action again. And they will want to. The divorced person is sometimes feared, especially by other marrieds who may feel their own marriage threatened. So, not only does the church have to extend healing love; sometimes it has to take a look at itself and expand its compassions.

The formerly married are beginning again. The goals that the marriage once had are gone. Sometimes this means that personal goals are gone as well. This is especially true for a woman. She may have to begin at a basic level in education and in work. Children make the situation more complicated, because their needs are expensive and continual. Some divorced or widowed will try to marry again right away, though it may not be advisable because "they are propelled by their own insecurity and fear of being alone. It is a mistake to jump into any kind of relationship until you have had time to adjust to your divorce and the new demands it has placed on you" (Jim Smoke, *Growing Through a Divorce,* Irvine, California: Harvest House, 1976).

The relationship with God and Jesus Christ suffers in the emotional intensity of losing or in the loss of a spouse. The divorced Christians began their marriages with every intention of them lasting. There was probably pretty good reason to believe it would. Therefore, the breakup of their marriages causes deep hurt. Then, in the healing process, it experiences a new vitality unsurpassed in quality.

The new singles then may have to begin their relationship with Christ and God again. They will probably have to confess many guilt feelings and resentments. There is also the big question: "How could this happen to me?" Most find God's heart big enough to accept them, and have found divorce and widowhood to be magnificent growing experiences. God can indeed restore the years that the locust has eaten (Joel 2:25).

The formerly marrieds' responsibility to their children, if they have them, complicates recovery. Children have expensive needs, both financially and emotionally. In divorce, many don't understand why Mom and Dad aren't living together anymore and want them to be together again. Single parents love their children, sometimes even more than before the split from or the death of the spouse. They try to give a lot of time and effort to their offspring who still need both parents very much.

Stages of Grief

One does not end something as emotion-laden as marriage without a whimper. All divorced persons experience shock as a first stage. They can't believe it's happening to them. They tried so hard and now it's over. They want to talk about the experience, and want to talk a lot. Friends must be good listeners, the kind who won't be harsh or place blame. They may have to listen to the same things over again. As the opportunity arises, friends should encourage the newly singled person to see the situation in perspective to provide a link with reality. The shock stage is a very necessary one, but the newly single person needs to be gently pushed out of it.

After the shock, sorrow and anger both set in. Anger is

necessary for healing because divorce is a betrayal, even if both sides are equally responsible. That anger needs to somehow be expressed, channeled, obliterated. If not, the divorced person will remain angry and never experience release from a bad marriage. The sorrow is experienced because of the good times the marriage brought. At times this grief may tempt the two people to get back together, since they are probably still attractive to each other. These reunions, however, rarely last.

The final stage, acceptance, only comes when anger and sorrow have gone their full round. It is an adventuresome time. Some people had married before they ever established a personal identity, and now they begin to experience "me" for the first time. They may discover talents and interests they never had time to explore before, or never felt they had the freedom to explore. Some don't know how to live alone, and require help in adjusting to all the responsibilities of supporting themselves because there is no one there to help make decisions. They may start ridding themselves of things that were part of their married life; they may move to a new apartment, change names, start going out, make new friends. It is a new beginning.

The Church and the Newly Singled

Fears and suspicions often keep it from aiding very needy people, but the church can take part in a person's new life if it chooses. Singles' groups provide a place for formerly marrieds to meet other singles. Many of these groups have very large formerly married attendance, sometimes as much as 50 percent or more. Even then, formerly marrieds sometimes hesitate to attend such a group, either because they think the group will be exceptionally young or they'll be the only divorced person there. One group leader jokingly promises inquiring divorced people that they don't have to wear the divorced sign all the other divorced people do. Other alternatives for meeting single people are slim. Bars, singles' clubs, and vacation tours just don't "cut it" when you don't want to get picked up or spend a fortune.

As a group of people, the church can show healing love in the abundance numbers brings. The emotions of death or divorce, when spread through the body and recognized by the pastor in the pulpit, give support and genuinely relieve the aloneness of the splitting of a couple.

A group of formerly married single adults in our church met for about two months to talk about their experiences and share their growth. They learned from each other and now know where to turn for support. When they accomplished what they had set out to do, they stopped meeting. Similar groups have arisen in other churches and have provided the same kinds of supports.

A particularly sore area for newly single people centers around church responsibility. One woman was asked to stop teaching her Sunday School class after her divorce because of the example she represented. She left the church too.

The divorced lose neither their brains nor heart when they leave marriage. They still have all their talents and gifts. They have not committed the unpardonable sin, yet the church will not let them forget. Too often it will not acknowledge the forgiveness Christ has already given. After a period of ailing and healing, these single people are as great a resource as ever.

Another of the church's responsibilities is to reduce the urgent push toward marriage, which encourages early marriage and in effect promotes divorce.

A full 50 percent of all teenage marriages (up to age 21) end in divorce. Many marry against good advice. But all faced the prospect of becoming second-class citizens at age 23 like the rest of the singles. One perceptive young divorcée remarked that the church "would rather see 1000 bad marriages than one premarital affair." So the church blesses the happy postadolescents and celebrates their nuptials, even while suspecting tragedy awaits in just a few years.

Britton Wood, of Park Cities Baptist Church in Dallas, Texas proposed: "Young adults need encouragement to become productive persons who know who they are, and to postpone marriage until they have been on their own for a few years." His reason: the very high rate of divorce among those who married when they were young. In his address to the Continental Congress on the Family, he further quoted statistics citing that the lowest divorce rates occur when people are married after age 25.

Divorce often follows the finest of intentions for marriage. Divorce has perplexed the church, and well it should. But even in divorce "God has called us to peace" (1 Cor. 7:15b). The church can be partaker with the formerly married in that peace. And if the church is to honestly establish ministry to the formerly married and maintain its ban on remarriage, it must begin to teach and accept the dignity and calling of singleness. Never-married people will profit from this shift of emphasis as well as those who ultimately find stronger marriages because of it.